VARIATIONS ON A MAIN COURSE

How to Create Your Own Original Dishes

JEAN CONIL and HUGH WILLIAMS

NEW ENGLISH LIBRARY

Also by Jean Conil and Hugh Williams and available from New English Library:
VARIATIONS ON A RECIPE
VARIATIONS ON A STARTER

First published in Great Britain in 1981 by
Judy Piatkus (Publishers) Limited

First NEL Paperback Edition November 1981

NEL Books are published by
New English Library
Barnard's Inn, Holborn,
London EC1N 2JR, a division of Hodder and Stoughton Ltd.

Reproduced, printed and bound in Great Britain by
Cox & Wyman Ltd, Reading

0 450 05204 4

CONTENTS

VEGETARIAN DISHES

FISH DISHES

BEEF DISHES

VEAL DISHES

PORK DISHES

LAMB DISHES

POULTRY AND GAME DISHES

OFFAL DISHES

COLD AND MADE-UP DISHES

APPENDIX:

Introduction

Variations on a Main Course is the third volume in the successful series *Variations on a Recipe*. The series shows you how to be less dependent on recipe books. It is a new approach to cooking which we believe to be long overdue.

The first volume in the series deals with a wide range of dishes, from soups to hors d'oeuvres and from main dishes to desserts. The second volume, *Variations on a Starter*, deals exclusively with dishes with which to begin a meal. The third volume deals with the centre-piece of any meal, the main course.

We have divided the book into nine sections to make reference as quick and easy as possible. There is a section on vegetarian dishes, one each for fish, beef, veal, pork, lamb, poultry and game, offal and, finally, a section of cold dishes suitable for using up left-overs and taking on picnics.

Each recipe follows the format of the previous two volumes. On one page we give the ingredients, preparation and cooking time, as well as the method of cooking, set out in simple stages. On the opposite page there are variations that you can make to each recipe, as well as chef's tips. These tips are little nuggets of information that Jean Conil has discovered or created during his long career as a French Master Chef and are of a kind seldom found in cookery books.

We have provided a wide variety of recipes, from the simple roast to casseroles, and more exotic dishes. Each recipe includes several ways of changing or varying the dish to suit your own taste and the ingredients in your larder. So from the specially selected basic recipes in the book, you can make hundreds more, and we hope you will soon create your own variations to suit your personal taste and budget.

With the increasing cost of wine, we have also included a section on basic wine-making. We have provided two recipes for wine, one for red and one for white, but here too there is plenty of scope for experimentation. We hope that this book, along with the other two in the series, will help you become a more creative cook, and that you will eventually be able to produce a culinary masterpiece from anything that you find in the cupboard. Use the book as a conventional recipe book by all means, but do become more adventurous, and try your hand at creating new dishes to suit yourself. *Bonne chance!*

Weights and Measurements

In listing the ingredients for each recipe, we have tried to make it as easy as possible for you to refer to whem shopping and cooking. The ingredient is followed by the quantity in convenient measurements like teaspoons and cups, as well as in imperial and metric weights. Hence oil is listed like this: **Oil 4 Tbs (2fl oz/50ml)**. The abbreviations "tsp" and "Tbs" are used for teaspoon and tablespoon respectively.

Since the introduction of metric measurements, recipes have had to include weight in both imperial (ounces and pounds) and metric (grams and millilitres) measurements. This poses a number of problems. The difficulty is in finding sensible equivalents; for example, one ounce is actually just over 28 grams. In the following table therefore you will see 1 oz = 25-30g. In many instances it does not matter whether you use 25 or 28 or 30. But think carefully about the dish in question and the particular ingredient if you vary the quantity too much.

WEIGHT

Metric	Imperial	Metric	Imperial
15g	½oz	450g	16oz (1 lb)
20g	¾oz	900-1000g	2 lb (1 kg)
25-30g	1oz	1½ kg	3 lb
40g	1½oz	2 kg	4 lb
50g	2oz	2½ kg	5 lb
75g	3oz	3 kg	6 lb
100g	4oz (¼ lb)	3½ kg	7 lb
150g	5oz	4 kg	8 lb
175g	6oz		
200g	7oz		
225-240g	8oz (½ lb)		
250g	9oz (¼ kg)		
275g	10oz		
300g	11oz		
350g	12oz (¾ lb)		
375g	13oz		
400g	14oz		
425g	15oz		

VOLUME

Metric	Imperial	US Cup
50ml	2fl oz	1/4
75ml	2½fl oz	1/3
	3fl oz	3/8
100ml	4fl oz	1/2
150ml	5fl oz (1/4 pint)	5/8
200ml	6fl oz	3/4
	7fl oz	7/8
225ml	8fl oz	1
275ml	9fl oz	1 1/8
300ml	10fl oz (1/2 pint)	1 1/4
	11fl oz	1 3/8
	12fl oz	1 1/2
400ml	14fl oz	1 3/4
	16fl oz	2 = 1 pint (US)
½ litre (500-600ml)	20fl oz (1 pint)	
750ml (¾ litre)	1¼ pints	
900ml	1½ pints	
1 litre	1¾ pints	

LINEAR MEASURE

Metric	Imperial
3mm	1/8in
5mm	1/4in
1 cm	1/2in
2.5cm	1in
4cm	1½in
5cm	2in
6.5cm	2½in
7.5cm	3in
10cm	4in
12.5cm	5in
15cm	6in
18cm	7in
20cm	8in
23cm	9in
25cm	10in
30cm	12in (1 ft)
35cm	14in
38cm	15in
45cm	18in
60cm	24in
92cm	36in

Equivalent Oven Temperatures

°C	°F	Gas Mark
110	225	1/4
130	250	1/2
140	275	1
150	300	2
170	325	3
180	350	4
190	375	5
200	400	6
220	425	7
230	450	8
240	475	9

SPOONS
(level unless otherwise stated)

Metric	Imperial
1.25ml	1/4 tsp
2.5ml	1/2 tsp
5ml	1 tsp
15ml	1 Tbs
30ml	2 Tbs (1fl oz)
3 tsp	1 Tbs
2 Tbs	1fl oz
16 Tbs (US)	1 cup (US)

BAR MEASURES

Dash	4-6 drops
Teaspoon	1/6fl oz
Tablespoon	1/2fl oz
Pony/liqueur glass	1fl oz
Jigger	1½fl oz
Wineglass	4fl oz
Cup	8fl oz

Physics and Chemistry

The best chefs and cooks don't need recipe books. They use well tried and tested formulae to make their creations. While we are not suggesting that you turn your ordinary kitchen into a chemistry laboratory, we are giving you certain guidelines that will help you to concoct your own dishes if you want to.

Some principles in creating a recipe are as follows:

Seasoning:
> Salt required is one per cent in weight of the total ingredients: e.g. 1 lb (450 grams) mashed potato needs 4.5 grams of salt (roughly one level teaspoon).

Spicing:
> 0.01 per cent of weight: e.g. 1 lb (450 grams) of minced meat needs a minimum of ½ gram pepper.

Wine in Sauce:
> A sauce containing wine should have no less than 40 per cent of the total amount of sauce as wine. But if you use fortified wines like port or sherry, reduce the amount of alcohol to 20 per cent.

Herbs:
> If you use fresh herbs you need ½oz (15 grams) per 1 lb (450 grams) of food. If you use the dried variety, cut the quantity to one eighth of an ounce of 4 grams per pound of food. **N.B.** Some herbs, like sage and thyme, are strong; perhaps add less.

Acidity:
> For a fish sauce you need acidity e.g. 2 Tbs white vinegar per pint of sauce (600mls) or the juice of one lemon.

Sweetening:
> Sugar content should be:
>
> For jams and jellies .... 66 per cent
> For jam sauce not more than .... 25 per cent
> In milk pudding not more than .... 15 per cent
> For cakes and sponges .... 25 per cent
> For light sponge .... 30-33 per cent
> In meringue .... 75 per cent
> For light meringue .... 50 per cent

In caramel and hard sweets .... 99 per cent
In sweet and sour sauces and chutneys .... 10 per cent

Balancing Cakes

- For a perfect cake you need a good patent flour. The calculation is based on the different quantities of eggs, fat, sugar and flour.
- A reduction in one liquid must be made up by another liquid.
- But if eggs are replaced by water, an aerating agent must be used with flour (Baking powder).
- 1 egg aerates its own weight of flour.
- 1 oz (25 grams) of baking powder aerates 1 lb (450 grams) flour.
- However for sponges the combination is different.
- If you put in two eggs you need 2 oz (50 grams) soft flour and 2oz (50 grams) caster sugar.
- This means that eggs weighing 4oz (100 grams) need 4 oz (100 grams) of solids to balance.

Milk and Cream

- Milk contains approximately ¾ oz (21 grams) of cream per pint (35 grams per litre).
- Single cream contains 18 per cent cream.
- Whipping cream contains 36 per cent cream.
- Double cream contains 48 per cent cream.
- If you whip double cream without adding ½ the quantity of single cream it will curdle and eventually turn to butter.
- If you have no single cream then add 10 per cent milk. Single cream by itself will not whip. However, if you add ½ oz (15 grams) gelatine to 1 oz (25 grams) sugar dissolved in 2fl oz (50mls) hot milk, you could blend it in to single cream and whip. After cooling this will give a reasonable result.

Thickening

- To thicken a sauce you need a minimum of 4 per cent starch.
- If you use a roux you need 5 per cent plain flour and 5 per cent fat.
- To thicken gravy you should add 24 grams cornflour.

Jellies

- To gel fruit juices you need at least ¾oz (22.5 grams) per pint or 4 per cent.
- To set jam you need 1 per cent pectin in the jam ingredients.

Colouring

- You can improve colour of sauces, jam, jellies or cake by the use of natural or artificial colourings:

  Green . . . Spinach juice or colouring

  Red . . . Cochineal colouring, raspberry juice, beetroot juice with vinegar

  Yellow . . . Turmeric, Saffron or egg yolks

  Black . . . Black treacle or gravy colouring

- It goes without saying that you don't usually put a sweet colour in a savoury dish, e.g. raspberry juice in a salad.

Table of Roasting times of Birds

With oven preheated to 400°/200°C/Mark 6

Black game ⎤ Guinea fowl ⎬ Pheasant ⎦	35-45 mins, according to weight
Quails (Browned first for 2 mins in a frying pan)	10 mins
Chicken 1lb	15-20 mins
3lbs	35 mins
5lbs	1 hour
Duck 5lbs	90-100 mins
Duckling 4lbs	45-60 mins
Turkey	15-20 mins per pound (after 1 hour reduce the heat to 375°F/190°C/Mark 5)

Goose	all small birds	15-20 mins per pound	
Grouse	must first be	15-20 mins	
Partridge	browned in a	20 mins	preheat oven to
Woodcock	little oil in a	15 mins	430°F/220°C/
Snipe	frying pan before	15 mins	Mark 7
Wild duck	being roasted	20 mins	

Garnishes

Chicken — grilled bacon, bread sauce, game chips, gravy, watercress

Pigeon — garden peas, carrots, and onions

Guinea fowl — grapes, apples

Duck — sage and onion, apple sauce, gravy, watercress, orange, cherries

Goose — apples, pears, liver and chestnut stuffing

Turkey — bread sauce, cranberry sauce, chipolata sausages, gravy, chestnut stuffing

Game birds — croûtons on which a little liver pâté has been spread, gravy, game chips, fried breadcrumbs, bread sauce, watercress.

All roast birds, particularly small ones, are best accompanied by a side salad.

Spinach and Mince Pie

Soya mince, spinach, and tomato casserole, topped with walnuts.

Ingredients

spinach (7lbs / 3kg)
onions sliced (8oz / 225g)
oil 3 Tbs
swedes sliced (8oz / 225g)
soya mince (4oz / 100g)
hot water (½ pint / 300ml) to hydrate mince
soya sauce 1 Tbs
wheat germ (1oz / 25g)
yeast extract 2 tsp
walnuts chopped (2oz / 50g)
tomatoes chopped (1lb / 450g)
salt and **pepper** to taste

Preparation time 45 mins   **Cooking time** 30 mins
Portions 4   **Calories per portion** 285

Method

1 Soak soya mince in the hot water for 30 mins.
2 Wash spinach thoroughly, remove stems, and then boil in
  salted water until cooked (4 mins). Squeeze out excess
  moisture, chop, and keep warm.

3 Heat oil in a pan, and gently cook onions without browning for 2 mins. Add all remaining ingredients except walnuts.
4 Cook for 5 mins, stirring occasionally.
5 Blend ingredients in a casserole dish with spinach and soya.
6 Sprinkle with the walnuts, cover, and bake for 30 mins at 400°/200°C/Mark 6, or until vegetables are cooked through.

Variations

A Omit soya mince, and replace with layers of cream cheese.
B Instead of walnuts, try boiled skinned chestnuts or peanuts.
C For a different texture, use green cabbage — if you do use green cabbage, a smaller quantity will be needed.
D To make this dish more filling add a layer of sliced or mashed potatoes to the soya and spinach mixture in the casserole. This will add more calories.

Chef's Tips

- if you use frozen spinach which has been thawed, you will only require half the quantity given in the recipe. Warm the thawed spinach between plates over boiling water before cooking.
- do not be astonished at the amount of spinach needed in the recipe. It boils away to almost nothing. Do ensure that you have washed the spinach thoroughly — several changes of water may be required.
- beet leaves make an excellent substitute for spinach.

Vegetable and Coconut Pie

Mixed vegetables and coconut, blended with a white sauce, in a pancake pie.

Ingredients

peas fresh or frozen (8oz/ 225g)
baked beans 1 small can (5oz/ 150g)
onion 1 large, chopped (4oz/ 225g)

potatoes (4oz/100g)
chervil 2 tsp
curry powder 1 tsp
dessicated coconut 1 Tbs

Batter:

eggs 2 medium, beaten
cornflour 1 tsp
skimmed milk (5fl oz/150ml)

yoghurt 1 small pot (5oz/ 150ml)
dessicated coconut 1 tsp
vegetable oil (1fl oz/25ml)

Sauce:

eggs 2 medium, beaten
cornflour 1 tsp
skimmed milk (5fl oz/150ml)
yoghurt 1 small pot (5oz/150ml)

dessicated coconut 1 tsp
vegetable oil 2 Tbs (1fl oz/ 25ml)

Preparation time 20 mins   **Cooking time** 45 mins (if vegetables are pre-cooked)
Portions 6   **Calories per portion** 337

Method

1 Boil peas in salted water until cooked (8 mins). Drain and and set aside.
2 Boil potato for 20 mins or until cooked (if you have not got any, already cooked, that have been left over from another meal). Drain and set aside.
3 Make a batter by blending together flour, water, skimmed milk and eggs. Add parsley and seasoning.
4 Heat a little oil in a 6-inch/15-cm pan and cook some pancakes. There should be sufficient batter for 9-10. When cooked leave on a tray to cool.
5 Strain sauce from baked beans, and then mix together beans, chopped potato, peas, and chopped onion. Season with dessicated coconut, curry powder, and chervil. Set aside, in a bowl.
6 Make sauce: mix cornflour to a smooth paste with a little of the milk; heat remaining milk, add cornflour paste, bring to the boil and cook for 2 mins, stirring all the time. Remove from heat and stir in beaten eggs and yoghurt.
7 Add sauce to vegetable mixture in bowl.
8 Brush a 2½-pt/1½-litre pie dish with oil. Sprinkle some dessicated coconut on the base. Line the dish, both bottom and sides, with the pancakes, saving 2 for a lid. Fill dish with vegetable mixture and sauce. Put 2 pancakes on top.
9 Brush with a little oil, and bake at 350°F/180°C/Mark 4 for 45 mins.
10 Turn out onto a warmed dish and serve hot or cold.

Variations

A Add 4 sliced hard boiled eggs to the filling for extra nourishment.
B Instead of using pancakes to line the dish, use slices of bread soaked in melted butter.
C For a richer sauce use double cream instead of skimmed milk and yoghurt.

Chef's Tips

● if you are using up left-over vegetables in this dish, they can be reheated in the sauce, before being put in the pie dish.
● the pancakes for this dish should be quite thin.

Vegetable Risotto

Rice cooked with mushrooms and onion.

Ingredients

rice — long grain (8oz/225g)
butter for frying (2oz/50g)
oil for frying (2fl oz/50ml)
onion 1 large, chopped (4oz/100g)
mushrooms — white, sliced (2oz/50g)
garlic 1 clove
water (1pt/600ml)
bouquet garni 1
salt and **pepper** to taste
cheese — grated Cheddar (2oz/50g)

Preparation time 10 mins   **Cooking time** 25 mins
Portions 8   **Calories per portion** 511

Method

1 Heat, in a saucepan, the quantities of butter and oil
 allocated for frying. Gently shallow-fry the onion for 4 mins
 until soft but not brown. Add mushrooms and rice. Cook
 for 1 further minute, and then flood with water. Bring to
 the boil.
2 Simmer, with a lid on, for 17 mins.

3 Add the bouquet garni and garlic, and simmer for a further 5 mins.
4 Remove bouquet garni.
5 Pour onto a shallow dish, and sprinkle with grated cheese.
6 Brown under the grill, and serve.

Variations

A You can add more protein to this dish by adding 4 sliced hard boiled eggs or 4oz/100g shelled chopped walnuts.
B To spice this dish, add 1 tsp curry powder.
C Introduce other vegetables to the dish e.g. beans, peas, carrots.

Chef's Tips

- if you cook the rice in a saucepan, ensure that you cover with a lid, to prevent too rapid evaporation. Remember rice absorbs 2½ times its volume of water.
- to colour the rice add 1 Tbs of turmeric.
- if you wish to bake this dish in the oven instead of boiling, you can. Cook for between 17 to 20 mins in a moderate oven.
- make sure you use long grain rice or fat grain rice for this dish.

Nutty Potato Cakes

Ingredients

potatoes (1lb/450g)
peas — fresh or frozen (4oz/100g)
walnuts shelled (4oz/100g)
carrots raw, grated (4oz/100g)
eggs 2 medium
salt and pepper to taste
onion 1 small, chopped (2oz/50g)
flour (2oz/50g)
oil for frying (4fl oz/100ml)

Preparation time 15 mins   **Cooking time** 35 mins
Portions 4   **Calories per portion** 410

Method

1 Peel potatoes, and boil for 20 mins. Drain well and return to saucepan. Reheat to evaporate as much moisture as possible. Mash, adding no liquid.
2 While potatoes are cooking, boil peas in salted water for 5 mins. Drain.
3 Blend peas, walnuts, carrots, eggs, and onion with potato. Season and cool.

4 When cool divide the mixture into balls the size of an egg —
about 3oz/75g, and then flatten until they are 1in/2.5cm
thick.

5 Heat oil in a pan, pass the cakes in flour, and fry until hot.

6 Serve.

Variations

A Replace peas with baked beans.

B Substitute cooked chestnuts for the walnuts.

C Add 2 chopped hard boiled eggs to the mixture, in addition
to the raw eggs.

D Instead of mashed potato, use well-boiled rice, cooked for
30 mins.

Chef's Tips

● make sure the cakes are rolled in flour before frying.

● use old potatoes for this recipe — new ones will not mash
so well.

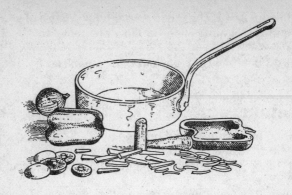

Chinese Fried Vegetables

Stir-fried mixed vegetables.

Ingredients

vegetable oil (4fl oz/100ml)
onions cut in rings, then strips (4oz/100g)
celery cut in strips (4oz/100g)
carrots (4oz/100g)
French beans cut in strips (4oz/100g)
bean sprouts (4oz/100g)
mushrooms white, sliced (4oz/100g)
green pepper 1 (4oz/100g)
red pepper 1 (4oz/100g)
salt and pepper to taste
soya sauce 2 Tbs (1fl oz/25ml)
garlic 2 cloves
ginger fresh (1/4oz/7g)

Preparation time 15 mins **Cooking time** 6 mins
Portions 4 **Calories per portion** 320

Method

1 Peel and wash all the vegetables. Make sure they are all cut in the same way — in strips about 2ins/5cm long and 1/4in/6mm thick.

2 Heat the oil in a large sauté pan, and stir-fry vegetables for 5 mins.

3 Flavour, and season with crushed garlic and soya sauce.

4 Serve.

Variations

A Replace the red and green pepper with the same quantity of pineapple, cut into strips.

B To the basic ingredients, add a few sprigs of cauliflower.

C Add some courgettes and cucumber — about 4oz/100g — also cut in strips.

D To add more protein to this dish, you can toss in some nuts.

Chef's Tips

- it is vital for this dish that the vegetables are not over-cooked. They must be crisp and firm.
- a mixture of butter and oil for the frying will improve the flavour.
- you can further vary this dish with a variety of herbs to your taste e.g. mint, fresh thyme, marjoram etc.

Cauliflower Cheese

With new potatoes and a mixture of vegetables.

Ingredients

new potatoes (1lb/450g)
cauliflower 1 medium-size
  (2lbs/900g)
carrots 4 medium (8oz/225g)

swede (8oz/225g)
peas (6oz/175g)
French beans (6oz/175g)

Sauce:

butter (1oz/25g)
flour (1oz/25g)
milk (½pt/300ml)
Cheddar cheese (1oz/25g)

egg yolks 2
salt and pepper to taste
sugar 1 Tbs (½oz/15g)
fresh mint 1 sprig

Preparation time 20 mins   Cooking time 30 mins
Portions 6   Calories per portion 260

Method

1 Peel new potatoes, add a sprig of mint, and cook in boiling salted water in a covered pan for 20 mins.
2 Drain and empty into a dish.
3 While potatoes are cooking, trim cauliflower, hollow out the stem, and cook in boiling salted water. Do not cover.

When cooked, drain well, but keep half the stock for cheese sauce.

4 Melt butter in a saucepan, and stir in flour. Cook for 1 min, then whisk in ¼pt/150ml cauliflower stock, and ½pt/300ml milk. Remove sauce from heat, season, then blend in 2 egg yolks and half the grated cheese.

5 Place cooked cauliflower in a shallow dish, and coat with sauce. Sprinkle with remaining cheese and surround with new potatoes.

6 Brown under the grill for 5 mins.

7 Boil peas for 6 mins in salted water. Drain.

8 Tip and tail French beans. Cut them into strips and boil in salted water for 10 mins. Drain.

9 Peel and cut carrots and swede into chips. Boil for 5 mins in salted water.

10 Surround the cauliflower and new potatoes with the other vegetables — peas, carrots, swede, and French beans, alternating the colour for better presentation.

11 Serve.

Variations

A Instead of cauliflower, use boiled green cabbage, with or without cheese sauce.

B Further supplement the assortment of vegetables by adding sliced celery, boiled for 10 mins and coated with cheese sauce. Alternatively use lightly boiled courgettes or marrow.

C For more protein, add such vegetables as baked beans or broad beans.

Chef's Tips

● a more aromatic sauce can be made by adding grated lemon and the juice of 1 lemon.

● cooking cauliflower without a lid on will ensure that it keeps its colour.

● undercook all vegetables for a better texture, flavour, and colour.

● new potatoes should always be cooked in already boiling water; old potatoes are brought to the boil in cold water.

Poached Salmon

With salad dressing and a fruit garnish.

Ingredients

salmon steaks 4 (6oz/175g each)
water (1pt/600ml)
wine vinegar (2fl oz/50ml)
bouquet garni 1
salt and **pepper**

Garnish

pineapple sliced or cubed (4oz/100g)
banana 1 small, sliced
cherries (2oz/50g)
cos lettuce (6oz/175g)
salad dressing (3fl oz/75ml)
mint a sprig
parsley a pinch

Preparation time 10 mins   **Cooking time** 10 mins
Portions 4   **Calories per portion** 307

Method

1 Clean the salmon steaks. Bring water, bouquet garni,
  vinegar, and seasoning to the boil in a deep metal tray

or fish kettle. Add the salmon, reduce heat, and simmer for 6 mins. Leave fish to cool in the liquid, and, when cold, discard skin and bones.

2 Place salmon on a flat serving dish; garnish with banana and pineapple. Mix herbs into the salad dressing, and coat fish evenly. Decorate with cherries, and surround fish with lettuce.

3 Serve, accompanied by boiled new potatoes.

Variations

A For a cheaper version of this dish, use a salmon trout, mackerel, or hake. When using hake or mackerel mix a little horseradish sauce into the salad dressing, and omit the fresh herbs.

B Replace bananas and pineapple with sliced cucumber and unpeeled slices of apple. Sprinkle with lemon juice to keep the apple green.

C Salmon stock can be flavoured with a bay leaf, chopped celery leaves, and a sprig of parsley, instead of a bouquet garni.

Chef's Tips

- the best salmon to use is Scottish or English.
- you can, of course, cook a whole fish; these are approximate cooking times for whole fish 8lbs/4kg 15-20 mins; 14lbs/7kg 20-25 mins; 20lbs/10kg 25-30 mins.
- salmon is in season between April and October (there are regional variations).
- serve fresh poached salmon with new potatoes and a salad.
- do not cook salmon on a high heat — this will cause the flesh to crack.

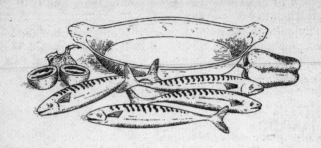

Simple Mackerel

Mackerel fillets baked in wine and vinegar.

Ingredients

mackerel fillets 4 (8oz/225g each)
onion 1 medium, sliced (3oz/75g)
tomatoes 2 large, sliced (3oz/75g)
red peppers 1 (3oz/75g)
loose sweet corn (3oz/75g)
bouquet garni 1
dry white wine (¼pt/150ml)
cider vinegar (2fl oz/50ml)
salt and **pepper** to taste
red chilli 1 thinly sliced
oil 2 Tbs (1fl oz/25ml)

Preparation time 10 mins   **Cooking time** 30 mins
Portions 4   **Calories per portion** 180

Method

1 Lay fillets of mackerel in a large shallow dish. Cover with all other vegetables, and pour in wine and vinegar.
2 Preheat the oven, and bake fish (covered with a lid or foil) for about 30 mins at 375°F/190°C/Mark 5.
3 Serve immediately, or allow fish to get cool in the juice and eat cold with a gooseberry sauce or purée.

Variations

A Instead of mackerel, use bream or rockfish, and cook in the same way.

B If chilli is too hot for you, use fresh or dried tarragon instead.

C Replace red pepper with 2 sliced peaches soaked in lemon or orange juice.

Chef's Tips

- for a professional appearance, soak mackerel, before cooking, in water with 5 per cent vinegar added. This will remove blood stains.
- sweet corn can be fresh, frozen, or canned. To remove fresh corn from the cob, remove outer covering, stand corn stem upward on a firm surface, and cut downwards with a sharp kitchen knife.

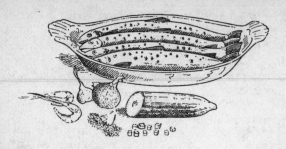

River Trout

In a prawn and onion sauce.

Ingredients

trout 4 (8oz/225g each)
seasoned flour (1oz/25g)

Sauce:

oil 2 Tbs
prawns with shells (4oz/100g)
onion 1 large, chopped (4oz/100g)
garlic 1 clove
tomato purée 1 Tbs (1fl oz/25ml)
curry powder a pinch
plain yoghurt 3 Tbs
salt and pepper to taste
cayenne pepper a pinch
white vinegar 2 Tbs
thyme a pinch
mint leaves

Garnish:

cucumber 1 peeled, seeded, and diced
shrimps peeled, cooked (4oz/100g)
capers pickled 1 Tbs
parsley chopped 2 Tbs

Preparation time 15 mins   **Cooking time** 20 mins
Portions 4 large   **Calories per portion** 230

Method

1 Wash and gut the trout, and leave in fridge while you prepare the sauce.
2 Crush the prawns, together with their shells, into a paste, and place in liquidiser with onion, garlic, tomato purée, and all other sauce ingredients, except yoghurt. Add water (½pt / 300ml).
3 Boil sauce for 15 mins. Strain, season, and blend in the yoghurt. Keep warm.
4 Pass trout in flour, brush with oil, and grill for 8-10 mins.
5 Place trout in a shallow dish, coat with sauce, and pour over all garnish ingredients. Reheat for 6 mins in oven, and, on serving, sprinkle with chopped parsley and a little dill.

Variations

A Use red mullet instead of trout.
B Omit sauce, and grill trout as in recipe. Sprinkle with flaked almonds and herbs of your choice, and reheat under grill until almonds are brown. Serve with new potatoes and a green salad.
C Use a little cream instead of yoghurt.

Chef's Tips

● fresh trout should have bright eyes, the gills should be a bright red colour, and not greyish brown.
● other points to watch out for when buying fresh fish: the scales should not be too loose, and the flesh should be firm and elastic; if you poke it, your finger should not leave an imprint; there should be no trace of an alkali or ammonia smell.

Cod Fish Stew

A satisfying cod and vegetable stew.

Ingredients

cod, all bones removed (1lb/450g)
celery 2 sticks (2oz/50g)
fennel (1oz/25g)
onion 1 small (2oz/50g)
carrot 1 medium (2oz/50g)
turnip (2oz/50g)
potatoes cooked (4oz/100g)
leeks 1 (2oz/50g)
garlic 1 clove, crushed
fresh mint a sprig
bouquet garni 1
tomato purée 2½ Tbs (2fl oz/50ml)
oil 1 Tbs
butter (½oz/15b)
salt and **pepper** to taste
water (2½/1½ litres
wholemeal bread 2 slices (4oz/100g)

Preparation time 15 mins   **Cooking time** 20 mins
Portions 4   **Calories per portion** 263

Method

1 Chop carrot and onion; slice all other vegetables.
2 Heat oil and butter in a large saucepan, and cook vegetables and garlic on a low heat for 5 mins.
3 Add water, bring to the boil, cover pot, and simmer for 15 mins.
4 Stir in seasoning and tomato purée; add bouquet garni, mint, and fish.
5 Return to the boil, cover pot, and simmer for 15-20 mins. Remove bouquet garni.
6 Chop the bread into cubes. Divide these into equal portions, put in bowls, and pour the stew over. Sprinkle with chopped mint and serve.

Variations

A Other fish can be used e.g. hake, coley, skate, halibut, bream, and haddock. Cook in the same way. But do avoid using an oily fish in this stew.
B For slimmers, omit oil and butter; just simmer the vegetables for 20 mins, and then proceed as before.
C Alter the vegetables to suit your personal taste, and to suit seasonal availability.

Chef's Tips

● you can liquidise the stew before pouring it over the bread.
● bread is used to add body; cooked rice or pasta is equally suitable.

Fillet of Sole

With grapes.

Ingredients

sole 4 fillets (3oz/75g each)

Stock:

fish bone and skin (8oz/225g)
onion 1 small, sliced (2oz/
  50g)
bouquet garni 1

carrot 1 sliced (2oz/50g)
celery 1 stick (1oz/25g)
water (8fl oz/225ml)

For cooking fish:

dry white wine (2fl oz/50ml)
lemon juice of half

fish stock (see above) (¼pt/
  150ml)
onion chopped (½oz/15g)

To thicken sauce:

egg yolks 2
cornflour 1 tsp

low-fat yoghurt (2fl oz/50ml)

Garnish:

muscatel grapes (4oz/100g)

salt and **pepper**

Decoration:

potato mashed (4oz/100g)

egg yolk 1

Preparation time 15 mins   **Cooking time** 25 mins
Portions 2   **Calories per portion** 308

Method

1 Wash fish. Boil stock ingredients for 20 mins, then strain and cool.
2 Tap the fish gently with a rolling pin; place in a shallow dish and season. Sprinkle with the lemon juice, and seed the grapes.
3 Put stock, wine, and chopped onions in a saucepan. Boil for 10 mins. Strain, and pour liquid over fish.
4 Cover fish with a lid or foil, and bake for 10-15 mins at 375° F/190° C/Mark 5.
5 When fish is cooked, strain liquid into a saucepan, and thicken with egg yolk, cornflour, and yoghurt, which have been mixed beforehand in a bowl.
6 Reheat sauce gently until it is the consistency of custard. Season.
7 Place fish on a flat dish with the grapes. Pipe mashed potato, blended with an egg yolk, round the edge. Bake for 4 mins at 400° F/200° C/Mark 6 to dry potato.
8 Pour wine sauce over and serve.

Variations

A Other filleted white fish can be cooked in the same way.
B Bake fish on a bed of spinach, and serve with a cheese sauce.

Chef's Tips

● if stock does not have sufficient flavour, add a chicken stock cube.
● make sure that the wine used in this recipe is dry — it will bring out the flavour of the fish.
● large muscatel grapes can be peeled as well as deseeded. There is no need to cook them before adding them to the fish. Canned grapes are readily available.
● Squeeze a little lemon juice on the fish just before serving it.

Prawn and Potato Curry

With a fruit garnish.

Ingredients

prawns peeled, cooked (8oz/225g)
onion 1 small, chopped (2oz/50g)
oil 2 Tbs (1fl oz/25ml)
red pepper (2oz/50g)
tomato purée 2 Tbs (1oz/25g)
water (½pt/300ml)
curry powder 2 level tsps
potatoes cut in cubes (8oz/225g)
salt and **pepper** to taste

Garnish:

mango sliced, fresh or canned (4oz/100g)
paw paw sliced (4oz/100g)
banana 1 small
lemon 1 cut in wedges

Preparation time 10 mins   **Cooking time** 15 mins
Portions 4   **Calories per portion** 180

Method

1 Gently fry onion in oil for 5 mins without browning. Add chopped pepper and cook for 2 mins; then stir in curry powder, and cook for 1 further min. Stir in tomato purée, pour in water, and add potatoes and seasoning.
2 Bring to the boil, cover, and simmer for 10 mins, until potatoes are just soft. Add prawns, and reheat for 5 mins. Check seasoning.
3 Serve and garnish with fruit.

Variations

A Instead of prawns, lobster, crab, or scampi can be used in the same way.
B Change the garnish: use sliced apple, pineapple, and seedless grapes.
C For a fruitier flavour, use pineapple juice instead of water in the sauce.

Chef's Tips

● to prevent the banana going brown, sprinkle with lemon juice.
● for a simple side dish, dice cucumber, mix in some low-fat yoghurt, and season to taste. A little crushed garlic will bring out the flavour of the cucumber.

Beef Stew

With a vegetable garnish.

Ingredients

beef stewing (1lb/450g)
oil or **fat** for frying (3oz/75g)
onion 1 large, diced (6oz/175g)
carrot 1 large, diced (6oz/175g)
celery 2 sticks, diced (3oz/75g)
garlic 1 clove, chopped
flour 4 Tbs (2oz/50g)
tomato purée 2½ Tbs (2fl oz/50ml)
bouquet garni 1
water (1½pts/750ml)
salt to taste
black pepper a pinch
ground mace a pinch
beef stock cube ½

Preparation time 15 mins   **Cooking time** 1½-2 hrs
Portions 4   **Calories per portion** 498

Method

1 Trim meat and remove surplus fat. Cut into 1-in/2.5-cm cubes.

2 Peel vegetables, and dice into ¼-in/6-mm cubes.

3 Heat fat or oil in a frying pan. First brown meat for 5-6 mins and transfer into a casserole dish. Then brown vegetables, and add to meat.

4 Sprinkle flour into frying pan; stir well, and add tomato purée, water, and stock cube. Boil for 8 mins, and strain over the meat.

5 Add bouquet garni, cover with a lid, and braise in a low oven at 325° F/170° C/Mark 3 for 1½-2 hours.

6 When cooked, remove bouquet garni, season to taste, and serve in a separate dish.

Variations

A At the last minute add a mixture of vegetables (peas, French beans, carrots, and turnips) which have already been cooked.

B To the basic stew add tomatoes (1½lbs/725g) skinned, seeded, and chopped, as well as 4 cloves of crushed garlic.

C Marinade the beef in red wine overnight, and then cook the beef in the marinade with half the quantity of water given in the main recipe. Garnish with button onions and mushrooms, which have been cooked for 20 mins with the meat.

Chef's Tips

● in all stews sprinkle 1 Tbs fresh parsley before serving.

● all stews can be flavoured with either red or white wine in the ratio of 20 per cent of the liquid used.

● all stews can be garnished with dumplings or snippets of fried bread.

14

Braised Beef Steak

Ingredients

beef topside, 8 thin slices (1lb/450g)
flour 2 Tbs (1oz/25g)
salt and **black pepper** to taste
oil (4fl oz/100ml)
onions 2 large, sliced (10oz/275g)
carrots 2 large, sliced (10oz/275b)
tomato purée 2½ Tbs (2fl oz/50ml)
water (1pt/600ml)
beef stock cube ½
bouquet garni 1

Preparation time 20 mins   **Cooking time** 2 hours
Portions 4   **Calories per portion** 581

Method

1 Blend flour with a little salt and pepper. Rub each slice of beef in it.
2 Heat oil in a frying pan, and quickly shallow-fry to brown the meat on both sides. Place the meat in a shallow earthenware dish.
3 Shallow-fry onions and carrots for 2-3 mins, and add to meat.

4 Boil water, stock cube, and bouquet garni for 4 mins, and then pour over meat. Cover with a lid, and cook in a moderate oven for 1½-2 hours at 375° F/ 190° C/ Mark 5.

5 Serve.

Variations

A For water substitute lager, stout, or Guinness. Omit carrots and double the amount of onions.

B Add tomatoes (1lb/450g) — skinned, seeded, and chopped — to basic recipe. Reduce water by half, and make up the difference with red or white wine.

C After frying vegetables add 1 tsp curry powder, then water and tomato purée, 2 cloves of garlic, 1 sliced peeled apple, and 1 Tbs sultanas. Serve with boiled rice.

Chef's Tips

● if, after cooking, the gravy needs thickening, blend 1 tsp cornflour with ½ cup cold water and add to boiling gravy. Boil for a further 5 mins to clear starch.

● the length of braising time depends on the thickness of meat, but in all cases low heat and slower cooking are advisable to tenderise the meat.

● so that the meat is as tender as possible, ensure that the lid covering the casserole dish fits tightly, in order to keep in the steam. If it does not fit properly, seal it with some pastry.

15

Sautéed Beef with Cream

Ingredients

beef tail end of fillet (1lb/450g)
flour 2 Tbs (1oz/25g)
oil 2 Tbs
butter (1oz/25g)
onion chopped (1oz/25g)
double cream (5fl oz/150ml)
lemon juice of half
paprika 1 tsp
salt and **pepper** to taste
parsley chopped 1 Tbs

Preparation time 15 mins   **Cooking time** 15 mins
Portions 4   **Calories per portion** 535

Method

1 Cut the meat into thin strips 2ins/5cm long and ⅓in/1cm thick.
2 Pass the meat in flour, and season with salt and pepper.
3 Heat half the oil and butter, and quickly shallow-fry the meat, stirring until brown. Remove and place meat in a shallow dish.

4 Sauté the onions in the remaining fat until soft, but not too brown. Drain off fat, then put back meat to reheat. Stir in cream. Season, and gently simmer for 5 mins. Do not boil.
5 Season, add lemon juice and paprika, and sprinkle with chopped parsley.
6 Serve with plain boiled rice.

Variations

A Use sour cream instead of plain cream, and add sliced mushrooms (4oz/100g) sautéed together with the onions.
B Add sliced mushrooms (4oz/100g) to basic recipe, and 2 pickled gherkins, cut in thin strips, as a garnish. Add 1 Tbs tomato purée to the sauce.
C Liquidise ¼oz/7g fresh ginger, 2 cloves of garlic, 2 Tbs soya sauce and ½ cup of pineapple juice. Add this mixture to meat before cooking. Season with a good pinch of cayenne pepper.

Chef's Tips

- do not stew the meat in its sauce. The meat, provided you do use fillet or sirloin, should be cooked through after being sautéed in the fat.
- you will get a crisper result after stir-frying the meat if you first roll it in flour.
- for an oriental flavour, roll the meat in a mixture of flour and curry powder before stir-frying it.

16

Beef Steak Pudding

A steamed suet pudding filled with steak and kidney.

Ingredients

beef top side (1lb/450g)
ox kidney (6oz/175g)
salt and **black pepper** to taste
ground mace a pinch
flour 1 Tbs
parsley chopped 1 Tbs
onions (1oz/25g)
Worcester sauce 1 Tbs

Suet paste:

flour (8oz/225g)
baking powder 2 tsp
salt 1 tsp
beef suet (4oz/100g)
water (2fl oz/50ml)

Preparation time 15 mins   **Cooking time** 2 hours
Portions 4   **Calories per portion** 527

Method

1 Cut beef into small cubes ½in/1cm thick.
2 Cut fat and sinews from kidney, and slice kidneys thinly. Wash with water and a little vinegar to remove smell. Blend the meat, with 1 Tbs flour, in a bowl.
3 Season, and add parsley, chopped onion, and Worcester sauce. Leave to marinade.
4 Prepare the suet paste: sift flour, salt, and baking powder. Rub beef suet into flour, add water; knead and then rest the paste for 10 mins.
5 Roll paste to ⅛-in/4-mm thickness, and grease individual pudding basins (¼-pt/150-ml capacity) or 1 large (2-lb/900-g) mould.
6 Cut out rounds of pastry to fit the tops of dishes. Fill each mould with meat, and cover with a pastry top. Seal. Wrap in greased paper and foil and steam for 1½-2 hours.
7 Turn individual dishes out onto plates and serve with a thickened gravy.

Variations

A Replace the kidney with the same quantity of mushrooms. Instead of steaming, bake in a pie dish in a low oven, 300°F/150°C/Mark 2.
B Replace kidney with diced carrots and peas.
C As A but flavour meat with 2 Tbs brandy and 2 Tbs sherry or port wine.
D Alternatively, you can serve the basic dish in one large bowl. In this case allow 3 hours for steaming.

Chef's Tips

● the smaller the meat pieces, the quicker the puddings will cook.
● to speed up the cooking process, stew the meat first, cool, and fill bowls as before. If you do this the flavour will not be as good but the meat will be rather more tender.
● other meats can be processed in a similar fashion to make all varieties of pudding.

17

Minced Beef Casserole

Ingredients

beef lean, minced (1lb/450g)
fat (2oz/50g)
onion 1 chopped
tomato purée 2 small Tbs (1fl oz/25ml)
flour (2oz/50g)
water (6fl oz/200ml)
salt and **pepper** to taste
ground thyme a pinch

Preparation time 15 mins   **Cooking time** 30 mins
Portions 4   **Calories per portion** 412

Method

1 Heat fat in a saucepan, and shallow-fry onion until soft but not too brown. Add meat and stir well.
2 Cook until meat is a light colour, then add flour and stir.
3 Dilute tomato purée with water and blend into the meat mixture.
4 Season, add thyme, and bring to the boil. Simmer for 30 mins, and then place in a shallow dish.
5 Cover with a lid, and braise in oven for 45 mins-1 hour at 350°F/180°C/Mark 5.
6 Serve with rice or mashed potato, and sliced boiled carrots.

Variations

A Add 1 or 2 Tbs curry powder to meat after it has been browned, and before adding liquid. Allow powder to cook with meat for 1 min before adding liquid. Garnish with 1 tsp dessicated coconut, 1 tsp sultanas, 1 diced apple. Serve with plain boiled rice.

B Blend into mixture 1 or 2 sliced green chillies, and 1 can of baked beans.

C Add to minced beef 1 cup of loose sweet corn and half a chopped red pepper.

D To transform this into a cottage pie, simply cool the cooked meat, place in a shallow dish, cover with creamy mashed potato, add a pat or two of butter, and bake in a moderate oven, 375° F/190° C/Mark 5, until golden brown.

Chef's Tips

● all minced beef recipes can be improved by using a cup of red or white wine, or by crumbling in a stock cube.

● the flavour is always improved by the use of such fresh herbs as oregano, mint, tarragon, chervil and marjoram.

18

Boiled Beef

Hot pot with mixed vegetables.

Ingredients

beef joint of thin flank, lean brisket, or silverside (2lbs/900g)
carrots 2 large (½lb/225g)
turnips 2 medium (½lb/225g)
cabbage 1 small (1lb/450g)
celery 4 sticks (6oz/175g)
leeks 4 medium (½lb/225g)
bouquet garni 1
onions 4 small (8oz/225g)
cloves 8
peppercorns 6
salt to taste
pickled cucumber or **gherkins**

Preparation time 15 mins   **Cooking time** 2 hours
Portions 6   **Calories per portion** 367

Method

1 Place the meat in a large pot, cover with cold water and
  bring to the boil. Skim off any fat that rises to the surface,
  and then simmer gently for 1½ hours, occasionally
  skimming off any scum.

2 Clean, wash, and peel vegetables. Tie the leeks in a bundle, stud each onion with 2 cloves, and cut cabbage in quarters.
3 After the meat has been cooking for 40 mins, add the carrots to the stock with the meat; then, 20 mins later, add the remaining vegetables and bouquet garni. Cook until tender.
4 Carve meat, and garnish neatly with vegetables and pickled cucumber or gherkins.
5 Serve with boiled potatoes.

Variations

A Serve dumplings with the meat. These are made by blending fat (4oz/100g) with self-raising flour (8oz/225g). Then add water until you get a soft dough. Divide into dumplings, each the size of a golf ball, and boil them in stock for 8-10 mins.
B Substitute knuckle of ham for beef, and introduce such other vegetables as peas in the pod or beans.
C A chicken can be cooked in the same way, but omit the turnips and carrots, and substitute peas and French beans.
D Cook three meats — ham, beef, and a boiling fowl — all together.

Chef's Tips

- ensure that you remove all the scum. This will produce a clear broth, which can be used for soups and sauces.
- cold beef can be reheated in sauces made from the stock.
- use a mildly pickled beef or salted ox tongue. But do take care to desalt the meat in cold water before cooking.

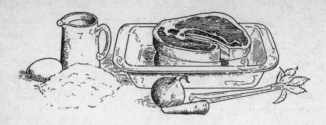

19

Roast Wing Rib of Beef

With Yorkshire pudding and horseradish sauce.

Ingredients

wing rib of beef (3¼lbs / 1½kg)

Gravy:

carrot 1 large (4oz/100g)
onion 1 large (4oz/100g)
celery 2 sticks (2oz/50g)

bouquet garni 1
salt and **pepper**
stock or **water** (1pt/600ml)

Horseradish sauce:

horseradish grated (1oz/25g)
water (3fl oz/75ml)
white vinegar 2 Tbs
   (1fl oz/25ml)

whipped cream (¼pt/150ml)
salt and **pepper**

Yorkshire Pudding:

flour (8oz/225g)
milk (¼pt/150ml)
water (¼/150ml)

eggs 2, beaten
dripping (2oz/50g)
salt a pinch

Preparation time 25 mins   **Cooking time** 1 hour 15 mins
Portions 6   **Calories per portion** 658

Method

1 To prepare, cut ⅞ of the way through the spine or chine bone. Remove the yellow sinew, and saw through the rib bone on the underside 2-4ins/5-10cm from the end. Tie firmly with string. Season the joint and place on a support of broken bones in a roasting tray.

2 Spread a little fat over joint, and roast in a preheated oven at 425°F/220°C/Mark 7 for 35 mins. Then turn joint over, and reduce temperature to 375°F/190°C/Mark 5.

3 Baste joint with juices from time to time until cooked. Cooking time is calculated at 15 mins per pound, and then an additional 15 mins.

4 On removing the joint from the oven, rest it for 15-20 mins.

5 Collect the juice and add to the gravy.

6 **Gravy making:** to the browned bones add sliced carrot, celery, and onion. Place roasting tray on top of cooker, over a gentle heat. Carefully remove surplus fat, and then add 1pt of stock or water. Boil for 15 mins and then strain. Season to taste.

7 **Horseradish sauce:** wash and peel horseradish root. Wash again, and grate finely. Soak in boiling water and vinegar. Leave until cold; then blend in whipped cream. Season.

8 **Yorkshire pudding:** blend beaten eggs with milk and water; add to flour gradually in order to obtain a smooth batter. Rest for 1 hour, while meat is cooking. Then heat up moulds with a little hot dripping in them. Pour mixture (about 2fl oz/50ml) into each mould, and bake for 15 mins at 400°F/200°C/Mark 6. This cooking is done, when the meat is almost cooked, in the top of the oven.

Variations

A Use a fore rib — it is slightly fattier, but cheaper.

B For a real treat try sirloin or fillet of beef — the most tender joint of all. Roast for 30-40 mins only if you like your joint underdone. Roast for 60 mins if you prefer it medium, and 90 mins if well-done. These times are for a 3-lb joint.

Chef's Tips

• for cheaper cuts, tenderise the meat: either hang for 4 days, or leave in fridge until a little sticky.

• for cheaper cuts, roast at a lower heat and for longer.

20

Braised Stuffed Shoulder of Veal

Ingredients

veal boned shoulder (2lbs/900g). Retain bone.
bouquet garni 1
carrots 2 large (8oz/225g)
celery 2 sticks (2oz/50g)
onions 2 large (8oz/225g)
tomato purée 6 Tbs (3oz/75g)
vegetable oil (3fl oz/75ml)
butter (1oz/25g)
salt and **pepper** to taste
water or **white wine** (¾pt/450ml)
Stuffing: see Variations

Preparation time 18 mins   **Cooking time** 1½ hours
Portions 8   **Calories per portion** 275

Method

1 In space where bone was, insert stuffing of your choice, and sew up the opening using string and a trussing needle.
2 Season meat on the outside and rub with plenty of oil and butter.

3 Cut carrots, celery, and onions into thick chunks, and place in the bottom of a shallow casserole dish, together with the chopped bone.
4 Heat a little oil in a large pan, and brown meat all over for 10 mins. Place joint on top of bone and vegetables and add water or white wine, tomato purée, and bouquet garni. Bring to the boil.
5 Cover with a lid and braise in oven for 1½ hours at 350° F/ 180° C/ Mark 5.
6 When cooked, remove meat and thicken gravy with 1 tsp cornflour blended with 1 cup of water. Cook for 5 mins, season, and strain.
7 Serve gravy with meat or separately.

Variations

A **Stuffing:** 1 large onion chopped and fried for 2 mins, blended with pork sausage meat (8oz/225g) and diced, soaked, uncooked apricots (4oz/100g). Add an egg and breadcrumbs (2oz/50g). Mix all ingredients together. Season with salt and pepper.
B **Stuffing:** same as stuffing A but replace apricots with the same quantity of diced bacon and white mushrooms.
C **Stuffing:** same as stuffing A but replace apricots with same amount of cooked spinach and ham (2oz/50g).

Chef's Tips

- the gravy made from the joint can also be used to accompany escalopes of veal.
- the same stuffing technique applies to other meat e.g. shoulder of lamb or pork can be stuffed in the same way.

21

Veal Cordon Bleu

Fried veal, ham, and cheese 'sandwiches'.

Ingredients

cushion of veal (1lb/450g)
cooked ham 8 thin slices (4oz/100g)
gruyère cheese 8 thin slices (4oz/100g)
flour 2 Tbs (1oz/25g)
salt and **pepper** to taste
egg 1 medium, beaten
white breadcrumbs (2oz/50g)
oil for frying (5fl oz/150ml)
tomato sauce (½pt/300ml) — see *Variations on a Recipe* p.18.

Preparation time 20 mins   **Cooking time** 5/6 mins
Portions 4   **Calories per portion** 774

Method

1 Trim veal and cut into 8 slices. Flatten them out by placing them between polythene sheets and hitting them with a wetted wooden mallet. Take care not to tear the meat.
2 Place a slice of ham and a slice of cheese on 4 of the veal slices. Cover with another slice of veal. Press the slices of veal in each sandwich firmly together.

3 Pass each 'sandwich' in seasoned flour, and then in beaten egg, and, finally, in white breadcrumbs.
4 Heat oil and shallow-fry the 'sandwiches' until golden brown.
5 Drain well and serve.

Variations

A The filling can be modified according to your own taste- although Gruyère cheese is best, any kind of hard cheese will do. Try sliced raw mushrooms or cooked leaf spinach instead of ham.
B With tougher or older veal, mince the meat, and divide into 8 balls. Flatten them into thin escalopes, and proceed as in the basic recipe.

Chef's Tips

- garnish this dish with a vegetable such as celery, leeks, or cauliflower, coated with a cream, tomato, or wine sauce.
- make sure that the 2 veal escalopes are well sealed on each side in order to prevent cheese from melting out during frying.
- avoid deep-frying this dish — remember only the thin slices of veal need to be cooked.

22

Veal Olives

Stuffed escalopes in a vegetable sauce.

Ingredients

veal lean, from leg or shoulder (1lb/450g)
pork or **beef** finely minced (4oz/100g)
onion chopped (1oz/25g)
egg 1, beaten
breadcrumbs (2oz/50g)
salt and **pepper** to taste
vegetable fat (4oz/100g)

Sauce:

carrot 1 small (2oz/50g)
onion 1 small (2oz/50g)
bacon streaky (2oz/50g)
celery 2 sticks (2oz/50g)
bouquet garni 1
flour 2 Tbs (1oz/25g)
tomato purée 2½ Tbs (1fl oz/25 ml)
water or **wine** (1½pts/900ml)

Preparation time 15 mins　**Cooking time** 1½ hours
Portions 4　**Calories per portion** 644

Method

1 Cut 8 thin slices of veal, place them between sheets of polythene, and, with a wooden mallet, flatten them out slightly.
2 Pass each escalope in a little flour.
3 Prepare the stuffing by combining the minced beef or pork, chopped onion, breadcrumbs, and beaten egg. Season.
4 Spread some stuffing on each escalope, and then roll meat to contain the stuffing. Tie with string or skewer with cocktail sticks.
5 Heat some oil in a pan, and shallow-fry the veal olives for 4-5 mins until brown all over, and then transfer them to a shallow dish.
6 Next prepare the sauce: dice the vegetables and bacon, and shallow-fry for 2-3 mins. Sprinkle in flour to absorb surplus fat, and then gradually add water or wine, stirring constantly. Lastly add tomato purée and boil for 10 mins.
7 Pour the sauce over the meat, cover with a lid and bake for 1 hour at 350° F/ 180° C/ Mark 4.
8 When cooked, remove string or skewers from escalopes, and transfer meat to a clean dish. Strain sauce into a saucepan, season, and boil for 5 mins. Pour over meat and serve.

Variations

A Any meat cut into thin slices can be used for this dish e.g. ham or beef.
B The stuffing can be varied by using pork sausage meat and combining it with a quarter of its own weight of raw liver.
C After cooking, cover the escalopes in pastry, and turn into a pie.

Chef's Tips

● instead of water, try using a stock to cook the meat in — it will give more flavour.
● if you cook the meat in wine, use sherry or madeira, a white wine, or vermouth.

23

Veal Escalope

Fried in egg and breadcrumbs.

Ingredients

cushion of veal (1lb/450g)
flour 2 Tbs (1oz/25g)
salt and **pepper** to taste
egg 1 medium, beaten
white breadcrumbs (2oz/50g)
oil for frying (3fl oz/75ml)
butter (2oz/50g)
brown sauce (6fl oz/180ml) — see *Variations on a Recipe* p.16

Preparation time 10 mins   **Cooking time** 4 mins
Portions 4   **Calories per portion** 539

Method

1 Remove any sinews from the meat. Cut veal into 4 even slices.
2 Place pieces of meat between polythene sheets, and gently hit with a wooden mallet to flatten them out.
3 Pass each escalope in seasoned flour, then in beaten egg, and, finally, coat with breadcrumbs.
4 Heat the oil in a pan, and quickly shallow-fry for 3-4 mins. Drain and place on a separate plate or dish.

5 Heat butter in a clean pan, and, as soon as it starts to froth, pour over each escalope.

6 While escalopes are cooking, make the brown sauce, and serve separately.

Variations

A The classic Viennese Schnitzel is made in very much the same way. Ensure that the escalopes are as thin as possible, and cook as described in the main recipe. Serve with a peeled slice of lemon, an anchovy fillet, 1 tsp capers, 1 olive, and half a chopped hard boiled egg per portion. Add some lemon juice to the batter poured over the escalope. Serve with sauté potatoes

B To do this dish Italian-style, cook in the same way but serve it with cooked spaghetti, tossed in butter with Parmesan cheese, and blended with strips of cooked ham, tongue, and sliced mushrooms. Serve with a little brown sauce.

Chef's Tips

● veal is best in the months from May to September. The best meat comes from animals that have been only milk fed. The flesh should be pale pink, firm, and slightly moist, and the bones should be a pinkish white. The fat should be white, and fat deposits in the kidney should smell sweet.

● the best cuts for escalopes are taken from the cushion — equivalent to topside in beef. When cutting escalopes, cut against the grain of the meat, and then thin them down with a mallet.

24

Veal Stew

With tomatoes and peppers.

Ingredients

veal from neck or breast (2lbs/900g)
seasoned flour (2oz/50g)
oil (4fl oz/100ml)
carrots 2 medium, diced (6oz/175g)
onions 2 medium, diced (6oz/175g)
celery 2 sticks, diced (2oz/50g)
bacon 2 rashers, diced (2oz/50g)
garlic 2 cloves, crushed
bouquet garni 1
tomato purée 8 Tbs (4oz/100g)
water (½pt/300ml)
white wine (¼pt/150ml
fresh tomatoes (1lb/450g)
red peppers 2 (½lb/225g)
salt and **pepper** to taste

Preparation time 25 mins **Cooking time** 1½ hours
Portions 8 **Calories per portion** 349

Method

1 Remove any excess sinews, cut meat into approximately 1-in/2.5-cm pieces and roll in seasoned flour.
2 Heat oil in a pan and then brown meat. Cover with a lid and, after 8 mins, transfer meat into a casserole dish — preferably a heavy metal one.
3 Shallow-fry the vegetables and bacon for 5 mins and then add to meat, together with garlic and the bouquet garni.
4 Stir in tomato purée, water, and wine, together with the chopped fresh tomatoes and chopped red peppers.
5 Bring to the boil and simmer gently for 1½ hours. Season and remove bouquet garni. Remove excess fat.
6 Serve in a clean shallow dish with a good sprinkling of parsley, mint, and tarragon.

Variations

A To produce a brown stew, omit fresh tomatoes and peppers, but add 1 beef stock cube, and use red wine instead of white.
B Omit red peppers, and substitute the same quantity of sliced mushrooms, which must be added 10 mins before veal is taken out of the oven.
C To change this into a creamy fricassee, do not brown meat too much, omit tomato purée and fresh tomatoes. Replace wine with the same quantity of cream, added at the last minute. Increase quantity of water to 1pt/600ml.
Garnish with whole small button onions, and baby white mushrooms, added at the last minute.

Chef's Tips

● to make an even richer fricassee, blend 2 egg yolks with double the quantity of double cream, which you add to the white sauce, away from the heat, at the last minute.

25

Braised Veal Sweetbreads

In a Madeira sauce.

Ingredients

heart-shaped sweetbreads (1½lbs/720g)
carrots 2 large, sliced
onion 1 large, sliced
bouquet garni 1
oil 4 Tbs (2fl oz/50ml)
flour 1 Tbs
tomato purée 1 Tbs
madeira 4 Tbs (2fl oz/50ml)
water (¼pt/150ml)
salt and **pepper** to taste

Thickening:

cornflour 1 tsp
water 4 Tbs

Preparation time 15 mins **Cooking time** 1 hour
Portions 4 **Calories per portion** 500

Method

1 Wash and soak the sweetbreads in cold water diluted with a little vinegar. Parboil them for 5 mins and refresh in cold water. Remove the skin membrane delicately.
2 Peel and chop the vegetables.
3 Heat a little oil in a pan, and brown the vegetables for 3 mins. Place them in a casserole or shallow dish.
4 Pass the sweetbreads in seasoned flour, and brown in the same oil for 2 mins. Transfer them to the dish with the vegetables. Add bouquet garni, tomato purée, madeira, water, and seasoning. Cover with a lid and braise for 1 hour in a moderate oven, 350°F/180°C/Mark 4.
5 Remove the cooked sweetbreads and transfer to a clean dish. Pour the liquid into a small saucepan and bring to the boil. Cook for 4 mins.
6 Add cornflour and water to thicken. Boil for a further 2 mins.
7 Check seasoning and then strain sauce over sweetbreads. The vegetables can be left in the sauce if desired.
8 Serve.

Variations

A Replace wine with a little cream.
B Once the sweetbreads have been parboiled and then cooked, they can be sliced, passed in flour, beaten egg and breadcrumbs, and fried in a pan. Serve with cooked asparagus tips or fried mushrooms.
C Blend diced, cooked sweetbread in a cream sauce, and serve as a filling in vol-au-vents.

Chef's Tips

● sweetbreads are glands and are of two types; the thymus from the throat is long and not as tasty as the pancreas, the gland from the stomach, which is heart-shaped and the best quality.
● sweetbreads are very nourishing, and are often recommended for people on a light diet.

26

Barbecued Pork Fillet

Pork fillets marinaded in a barbecue sauce.

Ingredients

pork fillet (1½lbs/720g)
soya sauce (2fl oz/50ml)
red wine vinegar (2fl oz/50ml)
honey 1 Tbs
brown sugar 1 Tbs
red colouring 1 tsp
garlic 2 cloves, crushed
cinammon a pinch
shallot 1 small, chopped

Preparation time (exc. marinade) 10 mins
Cooking time 30 mins   **Portions** 4   **Calories per portion** 275

Method

1 Combine soya sauce, vinegar, honey, sugar, red colouring, crushed garlic, cinnamon and shallot. Blend thoroughly, and marinade the pork in this mixture overnight in the fridge.
2 Take the pork out of the marinade, and place in a roasting tray. Save marinade for later. Roast meat at 425° F/220° C/ Mark 7 for 25 mins. Turn once or twice, and baste frequently with the marinade.

3 When cooked, take out of the oven, and serve with a salad of bean sprouts and boiled rice.

Variations

A Pork can be replaced by thin end fillet of beef, veal, or even breast of turkey.

B Vary the vinegar to produce a different flavour — cider vinegar, tarragon vinegar etc.

C When fillet is not available, cut a piece of loin in two, to produce two pieces of meat at least 2½ins/5cm in diameter. Proceed as in the basic recipe.

Chef's Tips

● it is important to cook this joint at a high temperature.
● ginger up the flavour by adding to the marinade some fresh ginger, liquidised with pineapple juice (½ cup).

27

Barbecue Spare Ribs

Spare ribs roasted in a barbecue sauce.

Ingredients

pork spare ribs (2lbs / 1kg)
sherry 1 wine glass (5fl oz / 150ml)
honey 4 Tbs (2fl oz / 50ml)
malt vinegar (2fl oz / 50ml)
tabasco 8 drops
mixed spices 1 tsp
soya sauce (2fl oz / 50ml)
garlic 2 cloves crushed
ginger 1 Tbs fresh, peeled
onion 1 small, chopped (2oz / 50g)
tomato purée 5 Tbs (3fl oz / 75ml)

Preparation time 10 mins   **Cooking time** 45 mins-1 hour
Portions 4   **Calories per portion** 525

Method

1 Simmer spare ribs in water for 20 mins. Drain well.
2 Liquidise all other ingredients.
3 Place spare ribs in a shallow roasting tray. Cover with the sauce. Bake in oven for 25 to 35 mins at 400°F / 200°C / Mark 6, basting frequently.
4 Serve with bean-shoot salad and boiled noodles.

Variations

A Spare ribs can be replaced by middle-neck cutlets of lamb.

B Breast of lamb or belly of pork can also be prepared in the same way, as can pieces of thin flank of beef.

C Alternatively, cook chicken drumsticks with the same or a similar sauce. Serve with boiled rice.

Chef's Tips

● try introducing fruit juices into the marinade — this can also help to tenderise the meat.

● if you do not like sherry, use some other form of alcohol — preferably fortified wine of some sort.

28

Sweet and Sour Pork Chops

Pork chops deep-fried in batter and served with a sweet and sour sauce.

Ingredients

pork chops 4 large (2lbs/900g)
flour 1 Tbs
egg 1, beaten
self-raising flour (2oz/50g)
water ½ cup (4fl oz/100ml)
onion 1 medium, chopped (3oz/75g)
green pepper 1 (3oz/75g)
oil for frying
salt to taste

Sauce:

cornflour 1½ Tbs (¾oz/20g)
water 4 Tbs
wine vinegar 3 Tbs (2fl oz/50ml)
sugar 2½ Tbs (1½oz/40g)
orange juice 3 Tbs (2fl oz/50ml)
sherry 3 Tbs (2fl oz/50ml)

soya sauce 2 Tbs (1½fl oz/40ml)
tomato purée 2 Tbs (1½fl oz/40ml)

Preparation time 15 mins   **Cooking time** 20-30 mins
Portions 4   **Calories per portion** 617

Method

1 Trim meat, and cut into cubes ¾in/2cm thick. Rub meat in flour and salt. Shake off any surplus flour.
2 Prepare a batter by blending the egg and water, and then stir in flour until the mixture is smooth.
3 Combine all the sauce ingredients in a bowl. Chop onion and cut pepper into strips, and leave on one side.
4 Heat the oil in a pan, and deep-fry the pieces of pork, after dipping them in the batter. Cook for 3-4 mins until they are brown. Drain on absorbent paper.
5 Heat 2 Tbs oil in a pan, and shallow-fry onions and pepper for 1 min; then add sauce ingredients, and boil for 6 mins.
6 Add cooked pork pieces, and reheat for 3 mins.
7 Check seasoning and serve.

Variations

A If you do not like pork, use veal, beef, lamb, turkey, or chicken in the same way.
B The sauce can be varied in a number of ways. Try adding ½ cup of pineapple, cut into strips, and use red as well as green pepper, or, if you like a hotter sauce, add green chillies.

Chef's Tips

● instead of sugar, use honey — it gives the sauce a smoother flavour.
● to make the meat more tender, boil gently for 20 mins, drain, roll in flour, then dip in batter, and fry for 1 min only.

German Pork Chops

Pork chops baked with red cabbage and cider.

Ingredients

pork chops 4 (2lbs/900g)
salt and **pepper** to taste
sugar 1 tsp
oil (3fl oz/75ml)
flour (1oz/25g)

Garnish:

red cabbage ½ (1lb/450g)
cider vinegar (5fl oz/150ml)
apples 2 large (8oz/225g)

onion.
demarara sugar.

Preparation time 10 mins   **Cooking time** 35-40 mins
Portions 4   **Calories per portion** 525

Method

1 Trim the chops and season with salt, pepper, and sugar.
   Roll in the flour.
2 Heat oil in a pan, and shallow-fry chops until brown —
   about 3 mins on each side.

3 Place in a shallow dish, cover with shredded red cabbage and pieces of apple. Pour cider vinegar over. Cover with a lid and bake for 25 to 35 mins at 375° F/ 190° C/ Mark 5.

4 Serve with baked potatoes in their jackets.

Variations

A Substitute veal chops for pork chops.

B Replace red cabbage with white cabbage. Omit cider vinegar, and replace with sour cream (5fl oz/150ml) and caraway seeds (1 tsp), added 5 mins before meat is cooked.

C Omit cabbage, and replace with the same quantity of peas and apples. Flavour with a little white wine, and a pinch of cinammon.

Chef's Tips

- it is important to maintain sufficient moisture during baking, so remember to keep dish covered.
- use cooking apples for this dish — perhaps Bramleys.

30

Pork and Egg Pie

Ingredients

flour (1lb/450g)
eggs 9
pork sausage meat (1½lb/720g)
margarine (½lb/225g)
chopped parsley 1 Tbs
salt ½ tsp
egg yolk 1, beaten
lard (1oz/25g)
black pepper a pinch

Preparation time 25 mins   **Cooking time** 40-50 mins
Portions 10   **Calories per portion** 451

Method

1 Rub the flour and margarine together in a bowl. Break in
  2 eggs, and add 1 or 2 Tbs water. Blend well.
2 Knead the mixture until smooth, roll it into a ball and cool
  in fridge for 30 mins.
3 Hard boil 5 eggs for 10 mins, shell, and keep in cold water.
4 Combine sausage meat with 2 eggs and herbs and seasoning.
5 Remove dough from fridge, cut in half, and roll out each
  piece to a rectangle ¼in/5mm thick.

6 Place half the meat mixture along the centre of one piece of pastry and arrange the hard boiled eggs along the top. Cover with the rest of the meat.

7 Place the second piece of dough on top. Trim excess, and crimp the edges to seal. Brush all over with egg yolk.

8 Make leaves out of left-over pastry and decorate the top of the pie.

9 Grease a baking sheet with lard, and place pie on it. Bake for 45 minutes in a preheated oven at 350°F/180°C/ Mark 4.

10 Allow pie to cool and then decorate with sprigs of parsley.

11 Serve cold with salads.

Variations

A Replace the hard boiled eggs with diced cooked chicken (1lb/450g), blended with the sausage meat.

B Replace pork with lean minced beef, or use a mixture of the two meats.

C Replace eggs with ½lb/225g cooked ham, and ½lb/225g cooked veal, blended with the pork.

Chef's Tips

● you can spice this dish up by adding a little brandy, together with diced soaked apricots.

● you can also bake this pie, if you prefer, in a flan mould.

● add 2 Tbs fresh chopped parsley and 2oz/50g chopped onions, or 1 clove crushed garlic.

31

Boiled Gammon

A party dish for special occasions.

Ingredients

green gammon (15lbs/7½kg)

Preparation time 15 mins   **Cooking time** 3½-4 hours
Portions 40   **Calories per 4oz/100g** 140

Method

1 Soak gammon in cold water overnight.
2 Place in a large pot, and cover with fresh cold water.
3 Bring to the boil. Remove scum until liquid is clear. Simmer for 3½-4 hours.
4 Cool in the same liquid.
5 When cold, peel off rind.
6 Serve with pickles and new potatoes. Reheat in the stock if you want to serve it hot.

Variations

A Remove rind, but leave the fat. With a knife, cut thin lines in a criss-cross pattern on the fat. Stud joint evenly with cloves. Reheat in oven for 45 mins, basting occasionally with cider or white wine. Remove gammon from oven. In a bowl, blend brown sugar (3oz/75g) with 2 tsp each of mustard powder, ginger, and mixed spice. Sprinkle this over the meat, and put back in oven for 5 mins until golden brown.

B Serve with glazed pineapple rings or apple fritters, or with red plums.

C Glaze with honey, and garnish with pears, peaches, or apricots.

Chef's Tips

- the difference between ham and gammon is that the latter is cut from a side of pickled or smoked bacon. The ham is cut from pork and then pickled and smoked as a piece.

- a good joint will have no stickiness, no unpleasant smell, and the rind should be thin and smooth, and free from wrinkles. The fat should be white, and the flesh pink and firm in texture.

- a 3-lb/1½-kg joint will take about 1½ hours to cook. It is best to simmer the meat at 180°F/60°C in liquid. The meat will be even more tender if it is left to cool in its own liquid.

32

Saddle of Lamb

With a Brussels sprout sauce.

Ingredients

saddle of lamb small (2lbs/
   1kg)

dessicated coconut 1 tsp
oil Tbs

Garnish:

mushrooms sliced (1lb/450g)
carrots sliced (1lb/450g)

Jerusalem artichokes sliced
   (1lb/450g)
onion sliced (5oz/150g)

Sauce:

Brussels sprouts (8oz/225g)
loose sweet corn (4oz/100g)

pineapple yoghurt 1 small pot
   (5fl oz/150ml)
nutmeg a pinch

Gravy:

sprout stock (5fl oz/150ml)
chicken stock cube ½
chervil or mint a few sprigs

soya sauce 1 tsp
garlic salt a pinch

Preparation time 25 mins   **Cooking time** 1 hour 15 mins
Portions 4   **Calories per portion** 389

Method

1 Heat the oven to 400°F/200°C/Mark 6.
2 Remove fat and kidneys from meat. Skin and core kidneys
   and soak them in vinegar and water for 10 mins. Drain and
   slice thinly.

3 Heat oil in a pan, and brown saddle all over for about 10 mins. Remove from pan.

4 Sauté kidneys in pan for 3 mins and then remove.

5 Place mushrooms, onions, carrots, and artichokes in a large fire-proof dish; add kidney slices and then the saddle. Season well.

6 Cover and cook in oven for 30 mins, basting with juices.

7 While meat is cooking, boil sprouts with corn in ½pt/300ml of water, until sprouts are just tender.

8 Strain off the liquid and save. Add half the vegetable water to the meat pan, and cook meat, uncovered, for a further 20 mins.

9 Add remaining vegetable water to yoghurt. Liquidise this with sprouts, corn, and nutmeg.

10 Remove saddle from pan, carve, and keep warm.

11 Strain juices from the pan into a saucepan, add soya sauce, crumbled stock cube, herbs, garlic salt, and pepper. Bring to the boil and simmer for 15 mins. Strain and pour into a sauceboat.

12 Reheat liquidised sauce, season to taste, and pour over vegetables in pan.

13 Serve with the meat, passing the gravy separately.

Variations

A In place of saddle you can use fillet end of boned leg or a lean young boned shoulder with the fat removed.

B Instead of Jerusalem artichokes use a mixture of parsnips, swedes, and turnips, and use such herbs as dill, fennel, or coriander.

C Instead of sprout sauce, make an orange sauce, perhaps flavoured with a little port.

Chef's Tips

- when buying saddle of lamb, ask your butcher to cut two loins across the bone to form a short saddle. Tell him not to include chump chops, but that you will want the kidneys.
- to make more portions, the saddle could be boned and stuffed before cooking. In this case, allow a longer cooking time.

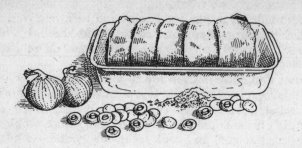

33

Stuffed Shoulder of Lamb

In a mushroom sauce.

Ingredients

shoulder of lamb boned (4lbs/2kg)
button mushrooms (1lb/450g)
onions 2 large, chopped
pearl onions (½lb/225g)
butter (5oz/150g)
flour 2 Tbs
egg 1, beaten
breadcrumbs (2oz/50g)
double cream 2 Tbs
oil 2 Tbs
stock (¼pt/150ml)
thyme a pinch
bouquet garni 1
salt and **pepper** to taste

Preparation time 20 mins   **Cooking time** 100 mins
Portions 10   **Calories per portion** 484

Method

1 Lay the meat, skin downwards, on a cloth. Open up the
   meat, and season inside with salt, pepper, and thyme. Set
   joint aside while preparing the stuffing.

2 Wash and chop half of the button mushrooms. Melt 1oz/25g butter in a saucepan, and fry the mushrooms and chopped onions until soft.

3 Liquidise onions and mushrooms into a purée, then return to a pan, and add flour. Cook for 1 min, stirring gently, then add cream, beaten egg, and breadcrumbs.

4 Heat the oven to 400°F/200°C/Mark 6. While oven is heating, place the stuffing in the joint, roll it up, and tie with string.

5 Place the lamb on a roasting tray, and brush with oil and 3oz/75g butter. Season and place in the oven.

6 After 30 mins reduce temperature to 375°F/190°C/Mark 5. Roast for a further 1½ hours, basting from time to time.

7 Melt the remaining butter in a pan, and fry the remaining mushrooms and the pearl onions until golden brown. Add bouquet garni, season, and pour in the stock. Cover and cook for 15 mins.

8 When the meat is cooked, carve in slices, and serve, surrounded with mushrooms and pearl onions.

Variations

A Vary the stuffing; use sausage meat, flavoured with herbs and onions, or use a fruit stuffing mixed with nuts.

B Omit the stuffing, and roast as for leg. Serve with a rich tomato sauce and some pasta.

C Instead of mushroom and onion garnish, serve a rich gravy, flavoured with orange liquer. After joint is cooked, sprinkle with brown sugar and return to oven for 2-3 mins to glaze it. Serve meat and gravy separately.

Chef's Tips

● when cooking a stuffed joint remember to cook at a slightly lower temperature, and allow 25-30 mins per pound.

● left-over meat can be minced, and served cold as a meat spread. Serve on hot toast with some chutney.

● a meat stuffing is best bound with an egg or two to improve the texture.

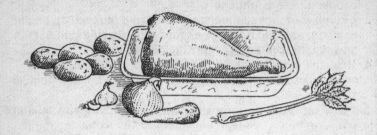

34

Roast Leg of Lamb

A classic dish.

Ingredients

leg of lamb (3½lbs / 1.7kg)

Gravy:

carrot 1 large
celery 1 stick
onion 1, medium
bouquet garni 1
water (1pt / 600ml)

Preparation time 15 mins   **Cooking time** 1 hour 50 mins
Portions 10   **Calories per portion** 169

Method

1 Remove any surplus fat, and tie up the leg with string if necessary.
2 Preheat the oven at 425°F/220°C/Mark 7. Place any surplus bones and trimmings in roasting tray. Season the joint with salt and pepper, and place on top of the bones. Spread a little beef or pork dripping on meat, and place in oven.

3 After 30 mins, start basting the joint, and reduce heat to 400°F/200°C/Mark 6. Cook for another hour or so, and baste every 30 mins.

4 When meat is cooked, place it in a shallow dish in a low oven, while you make the gravy.

5 Peel, wash and slice all the vegetables. Put the roasting dish containing the meat fat and juices on top of the cooker on a low heat. Remove most floating fat, leaving about 2 Tbs behind.

6 Add vegetables to roasting tray, and brown gently for 5-6 mins. Add water and bouquet garni. Boil for 15 mins. Strain, season to taste, and pour into a sauceboat.

7 Serve, accompanied by sauté potatoes.

Variations

A You can also pot-roast a leg. Cook at a lower temperature, 375°F/190°C/Mark 5 for 2 hours, and add a large carrot, 1 medium onion, and 2 sticks of celery in ½pt water or wine, 30 mins before the joint is cooked.

B Vary the sauces you serve with roast lamb — flavour the gravy with different herbs or serve with mint sauce or red-currant jelly.

C You can alter the flavour of the meat while it is cooking by pressing in some garlic before roasting, or scattering some rosemary about 30 mins before the meat is cooked.

Chef's Tips

- when roasting lamb remember to allow 20 mins per pound, plus 20 mins over.
- avoid buying half a leg; it is cheaper in the long run to buy a whole one.
- English lamb is better than other varieties; it has more flavour and is less fatty.
- if you are cooking a frozen joint, allow it to thaw out completely.
- if you have any meat left over, turn it into a shepherds pie, or moussaka, or curry; if you do not have enough left over for that, mince any left-overs and use them to stuff tomatoes, peppers, or marrow.

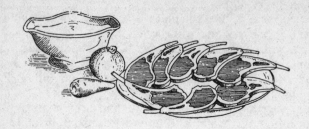

35

Lamb Cutlets

Reform-style.

Ingredients

lamb cutlets 8 (2lbs/900g)
seasoned flour (2oz/50g)
eggs 2, beaten

breadcrumbs (6oz/175g)
oil (4fl oz/100ml)

Sauce:

fat (1oz/25g)
flour (1oz/25g)
onion 1, chopped (2oz/50g)
carrot 1, chopped (2oz/50g)
beetroot 1, chopped
   (2oz/50g)
bacon 2 rashers, chopped

tomato purée 2 Tbs
chicken stock cube 1
water (½pt/300ml)
red wine (¼pt/150ml)
ginger a pinch
salt and pepper

Garnish:

hard boiled egg (white only) ⎫ each cut into thin strips of
gherkin 1 pickled　　　　　 ⎬ uniform size — 1½in/7cm
beetroot 1 small, cooked　　⎭ long × ⅛in/3mm thick
mushroom 1 large, white

Preparation time 25 mins　Cooking time 25 mins
Portions 4　Calories per portion 1405

Method

1 Remove bone from each cutlet. Trim surplus fat. Flatten them a little by placing each between polythene sheets and hitting it with a mallet.
2 Pass each cutlet in seasoned flour, then in beaten egg, and finally in breadcrumbs. Leave on one side and prepare the sauce.
3 Heat fat in a pan, brown the bacon, add vegetables, and shallow-fry for 5 mins. Sprinkle in flour, stir in tomato purée, and add water and red wine. Boil for 20 mins and crumble in a stock cube. Add ground ginger, check seasoning, and strain.
4 Add strips of garnish to sauce and reheat for 5 mins.
5 Fry the cutlets gently in a pan for 5 mins on each side.
6 Drain and dry cutlets, and serve sauce separately.

Variations

A Add a few crushed peanuts or almonds to the breadcrumbs.
B Make the sauce in the same way but add 2 Tbs vinegar for a more piquant flavour.
C Omit egg white in sauce. Replace with orange skin strips. Dilute in the sauce 1 Tbs orange marmalade and 1 Tbs of orange liquer or brandy.
D The lamb cutlets can form part of a classic mixed grill, accompanied by grilled bacon, kidneys, and sausages.

Chef's Tips

● you can make the cutlets even thinner by hitting them for a little longer with the mallet, and cooking them like veal escalope.
● try not to overcook; the meat tastes much better if not too dry.
● the cutlets can be marinaded in wine before cooking them.

36

Lamb Kebab

With a sweet and sour sauce.

Ingredients

loin of lamb (1½lbs/700g)

Marinade:

white wine (4fl oz/100ml)
oil 1 Tbs
white vinegar 1 Tbs
honey 1 Tbs
salt and **pepper**
chilli pepper a pinch
soya sauce 1 Tbs
cornflour 2 tsp

Garnish:

red pepper 1
green pepper 1
onion 8 small (6oz/175g)
button mushrooms 8 (6oz/175g)
pineapple 4 cubes
bay leaves 4
oil for frying

Marinade time 6 hours
Preparation time 20 mins   **Cooking time** 10 mins
Portions 4   **Calories per portion** 493

Method

1 Trim meat of any fat and sinew, and cut into 1-in/2.5-cm cubes.
2 Combine all the marinade ingredients, and soak meat in the liquid for 6 hours.
3 Remove meat and dry with a cloth.
4 Boil up marinade with a cup of water, thicken with cornflour blended with a further ½ cup of water to make a sauce, and simmer while cooking kebabs.
5 Deseed the peppers, and cut into squares. Alternate the ingredients on skewers — meat, pepper, onions, pineapple, mushrooms, and bay leaf.
6 Brush oil over, place on a metal tray, and gently grill for 8 mins until cooked.
7 Serve with sweet and sour sauce and rice pilaff.

Variations

A Vary the ingredients in the kebab. Alternate meat with cubes of lamb's liver or kidney, and change the vegetables. Add sausage and bacon.
B Omit the marinade, and, instead, flavour meat with a little Worcester sauce.
C Instead of making a sauce from the marinade, make a garlic and onion sauce to serve with the kebabs.

Chef's Tips

● loin of lamb is the most tender part of the animal, and requires very little cooking. You can use meat from the thick part of the leg, but, if so, soak overnight in pineapple juice to tenderise it.
● you can buy special kebab skewers which vary in length from 6ins–14ins.

37

Lamb Casserole

With haricot beans.

Ingredients

lamb lean meat from shoulder (1½lbs/700g)
fat or **oil** (2oz/50g)
bacon 4 streaky rashers, diced
button onions 8 (8oz/225g)
garlic 2 cloves, crushed
flour (2oz/50g)
water (1½pt/900ml)
bouquet garni 1
haricot beans dry (8oz/225g)
tomato purée 8 Tbs (4oz/100g)
salt and **pepper** to taste
oregano ½ tsp
parsley chopped 1 Tbs

Preparation time 20 mins   **Cooking time** 2 hours
Portions 6   **Calories per portion** 562

Method

1 Put beans and water in a covered casserole and bake in the oven for 1 hour at 350°F/180°C/Mark 4.

2 Heat the fat or oil in a large metal casserole. Shallow-fry bacon until crisp; remove bacon, and next shallow-fry button onions for 1 min. Remove them and keep in a bowl.

3 Brown meat in fat for 5 mins. Add garlic, and stir in flour. Cook for 1 min, and pour water over meat. Add bouquet garni, and simmer for 30 mins.

4 Add beans, tomato purée, seasoning, and oregano. Simmer in oven at 350°F/180°C/Mark 4 for 1½ hours. After 70 mins, add button onions and bacon pieces.

5 Scoop out any floating fat, sprinkle with chopped parsley, and serve.

Variations

A Instead of water, use meat stock, or half meat stock and half wine. This will give more flavour.

B When browning the meat add 1oz/25g paprika pepper. When nearly cooked dilute ¼ pt/150ml sour cream into sauce. Make some dumplings separately, and add to stew 10 mins before taking out of the oven.

C On browning the meat, add 2 or 3 Tbs curry powder. Serve with rice, sliced bananas, diced tomato and onion, wedges of lemon, chutney, and popadums.

D As B but omit dumplings. Decorate with olives and top with sour cream.

Chef's Tips

● instead of using meat which you cut into cubes, you can use lamb chops — allow 2 per person. This is slightly more expensive, but you will not have to cook it for so long. Reduce cooking time to 45 mins.

● add herbs 5 minutes before serving — the flavour will be stronger.

● to save time use a can of baked beans — added to the stew 5 mins before the meat is ready.

38

Irish Stew

Lamb stewed with potatoes, cabbage, leeks, and onions.

Ingredients

stewing lamb (1½lbs/700g) from neck, shoulder, or breast
potatoes (1½lbs/700g)
celery 3 sticks (4oz/100g)
onion 1, large
leeks (8oz/225g)
white cabbage (8oz/225g)
parsley 2 Tbs
button onions 8 (8oz/225g)
bouquet garni 1
salt and **pepper** to taste

Preparation time 20 mins   **Cooking time** 1½ hours
Portions 6   **Calories per portion** 435

Method

1 Trim and cut the meat into cubes. Remove excess fat and sinew.
2 Place the meat in a saucepan. Cover with boiling water, and boil for 5 mins. Pour water away, and wash meat.

3 Put meat back in saucepan, cover with cold water. Bring to the boil, and remove any scum until the liquid is clear. Add bouquet garni.
4 Peel potatoes evenly, slice and shred leeks, celery, cabbage, and large onions. Peel button onions.
5 After stew has been cooking for 30 mins, add all vegetables except potato and peeled button onions.
6 After another 30 mins, add potatoes, thinly sliced, and button onions, and cover with a lid.
7 Season with salt and pepper. Sprinkle with chopped parsley just before serving.

Variations

A Omit potatoes and replace with pearl barley (which has been soaked in water for 3 hours). Add some chopped turnip and carrot.
B Instead of lamb use mutton, and add other vegetables — peas, beans, fennel. Add 2 or 3 chilli peppers, and serve with couscous (wheat semolina). Cook couscous in meat stock — 1 cup couscous to 2 cups stock. Cook until all liquid has been evaporated.
C Add baked or haricot beans to the stew, omit leeks, white cabbage, and celery. Add lots of chilli pepper, and serve with corn on the cob.

Chef's Tips

● for a richer stew, add ½pt/300ml double cream when cooked. Reheat to boiling point and blend in 3 tsp cornflour for a thick creamy sauce.
● at the end of the cooking time, if there is any fat floating on the surface, scoop it off gently.

39

Mutton Moussaka

Layers of aubergines and mutton, topped with cheese.

Ingredients

mutton lean, minced (1½lbs/700g)
onions 2, chopped (6oz/175g)
garlic 2 cloves, crushed
flour (3oz/75g)
tomato purée 6 Tbs (3oz/75g)
water (½pt/300ml)
salt and **pepper** to taste
oregano or **ground mint** a pinch
eggs 2
aubergines 4 (2lbs/900g)
cheese grated (4oz/100g)
oil for deep frying

Preparation time 20 mins   **Cooking time** 45 mins
Portions 6   **Calories per portion** 517

Method

1 Slice the aubergines either across or lengthways. Sprinkle
  with some salt and leave for 10 mins.
2 Heat oil in a large saucepan, and brown onion for 2 mins,
  then stir in minced meat. Cook until brown. Add flour,

then blend in tomato purée, add seasoning and herbs. Pour in water, and simmer gently for 15 mins. Lastly, away from heat, blend in beaten eggs, and check seasoning.

3 Heat some more oil in a deep frying pan; wash salt off aubergines and dry with a cloth. Pass aubergines quickly in some flour and deep-fry for 30 secs. Drain on cloth or absorbent paper.

4 Line a pie dish 2ins deep x 8ins long (5cm x 18cm) with one layer of aubergine slices, then a layer of cooked meat. Repeat again, and top with a layer of aubergines.

5 Sprinkle with grated cheese, and bake in oven for 30 mins at 400°F/200°C/Mark 6 until golden brown.

6 Serve.

Variations

A A quicker way is to use cooked meat from a joint, but the flavour will not be quite the same. Reheat the cooked meat in a thick brown sauce.

B Instead of topping moussaka with aubergines, top with sliced boiled potatoes coated with a white or lemon sauce, with cheese on top. Cook in the same way.

C Top with cooked noodles blended with a cheese sauce.

D Make the moussaka with other minced meat — beef, veal, chicken etc.

Chef's Tips

● sprinkling salt on aubergines extracts some of the bitter juices.

● make sure the mince you use is best quality — too much fat will spoil the result.

● aubergines can be scalded for this recipe, instead of deep-fried. In this way the dish will be less fatty. Marrows can be used instead of aubergines. You can peel the aubergines if you want to.

40

Cornish Pasties

Lamb, potato, and onion in a short crust pastry case.

Ingredients

raw minced lamb (5oz/150g)
potatoes peeled and diced (4oz/100g)
onion 1 small, chopped (1oz/25g)
fresh parsley 1 Tbs
water 2 Tbs
salt and **pepper**
egg 1, beaten

Short crust pastry:

flour (8oz/225g)
lard (1oz/25g)
margarine (2oz/50g)
water 2fl oz/50ml or 1 **egg**

Preparation time 15 mins   **Cooking time** 40 mins
Portions 4   **Calories per portion** 438

Method

1 Rub fat and flour together, and add water or egg to form a dough. Roll to a ball.

2 Roll out to ⅛in/3mm thickness and cut rounds 5ins/10cm in diameter. You should get 4.

3 Combine all filling ingredients, and on each pastry round place 2 Tbs of the mixture. Wet the edge of pastry with water, and bring two sides upwards to seal. Crimp shut with fingers.

4 Place on a greased tray, brush with beaten egg, and bake for 40 mins at 300°F/150°C/Mark 2 until golden.

5 Serve hot or cold — if as a main meal serve with a green salad.

Variations

A Instead of short crust pastry use puff pastry, and cut the cooking time to 20 mins.

B Add chopped leeks and carrots to meat, or, perhaps, some chopped red pepper and mushrooms.

C Other meats can be used as well — veal, beef, bacon, or poultry.

D For a richer pastry, blend some lean raw mince with minced raw liver. Add 1 beaten egg, then add some chopped onion, and an equal amount of mushrooms, asparagus tips, and peas. Add 2 Tbs brandy, and leave filling overnight in a bowl in the fridge. Then proceed as in the basic dish.

Chef's Tips

● you can use part-cooked ingredients, for example some cooked potato, cabbage, or sprouts, but the result is better if the ingredients are fresh and raw.

● use frozen pastry if you want to save time.

41

Honey Duckling

With grapefruit and orange.

Ingredients

fresh duckling (5lbs/2½kg)
salt to taste
onion 1 medium (3oz/75g)

carrot 1 medium (3oz/75g)
celery 2 sticks (2oz/50g)
oil 1 Tbs

Fruit Sauce:

white vinegar 2 Tbs
cornflour (½oz/15g)
orange and **grapefruit juice**
  mixed (¼pt/150ml)
sugar 1 Tbs
tomato purée 1 Tbs

dry sherry (¼pt/150ml)
water (¼pt/150ml)
chicken stock cube 1
garlic 1 clove
bouquet garni 1
fresh mint a pinch

Glaze:

white vinegar 2 Tbs
cold water (¼pt/150ml)
liquid honey (4½oz/125g)

orange 1
grapefruit 1

Preparation time 15 mins   **Cooking time** 2 hours
Portions 4   **Calories per portion** 585

Method

1 Heat the oven to 200°F/400°C/Mark 6. Wash the duck, drain, and dry. Season with salt. Scald neck, winglets, and gizzard, and place in a roasting pan.

2 Peel and quarter the carrot and onion, chop celery, and put in roasting pan on top of giblets.

3 Brush duck with oil, and place, breast up, on top of vegetables. Roast for 35 mins then reduce heat to 350°F/180°C/Mark 4. Cook for a further hour, turning until evenly browned, and baste from time to time. When cooked, drain off any excess fat, and keep the duck warm. Retain juices in roasting tray.

4 For the sauce, place roasting tray on a ring, and boil down ingredients for 5 mins. While you are doing this, cook sugar in a corner until it caramelises. Then pour in fruit juice and vinegar, and stir in tomato purée, wine, water, and stock cube. Cook for 2 mins. Add crushed garlic, mint, and the bouquet garni; cook for a further 15 mins.

5 For the glaze, boil honey and vinegar in a pan and pour over the warm duck. Return to oven for 5 mins.

6 Blend cornflour with remaining cold water and pour into sauce. Leave to clear for 5 mins, then strain and season.

7 Peel the rind of the orange and grapefruit. Cut into short thin strips. Boil in water for 10 mins and then add to sauce. Skin fruit segments, and reserve for garnish.

8 Place duck on a dish. Pour some sauce over duck, and the rest into a sauceboat. Serve garnished with fruit segments.

Variations

A Change the garnish to peaches or red morello cherries.

B Prepare the sauce without fruit juice, and garnish with baked or fried quartered apples.

Chef's Tips

- a good duck has a clean smell, its feet are bright yellow and there should be plenty of flesh on the breast.
- save the fat from the roasting — it is excellent to use when frying potatoes.
- to flavour sauce add some alcohol.

42

Fried Breast of Turkey Escalopes

With pineapple in a sweet and sour sauce.

Ingredients

turkey 4 thick slices from breast (4oz/100g each)
flour, seasoned 4 Tbs (2oz/50g)
oil 8 Tbs (4fl oz/100ml)
pineapple slices 4, fresh or canned

Sweet and sour sauce:

white vinegar 1 Tbs
red chilli 1, chopped
honey 1 Tbs
garlic 1 clove
onion 1 small, chopped
fresh ginger 1 small piece
soya sauce 1 Tbs
cornflour 2 tsp
cold water ½ cup (4fl oz/100ml)

Preparation time 20 mins   **Cooking time** 12 mins
Portions 4   **Calories per portion** 450

Method

1 Remove skin from turkey and place each slice between two sheets of polythene. Hit gently with a wooden mallet until the slices are thin. Wet the turkey slightly in order to make this operation easier. Dry meat, and dust with seasoned flour.
2 Heat oil, and quickly fry escalopes on both sides for 4-5 mins. Keep them warm in a shallow dish. In the same oil, fry pineapple until golden, and place on top of escalopes.
3 Boil up all sauce ingredients for 4 mins. Liquidise, and reboil for 2 mins. Thicken by adding a slurry of cornflour and water. Season. Serve sauce separately.
4 Serve with a garnish of plain boiled rice or sweetcorn.

Variations

A Omit pineapple. Dip escalopes in beaten egg and breadcrumbs, and pan fry. Garnish with a slice of lemon and serve with sauté potatoes.
B Serve escalopes with a mushroom sauce to which ¼pt/ 150ml of cream has been added.
C Place a slice of thin cooked ham over escalopes. Roll and tie with string. Pass in flour, beaten egg, and breadcrumbs and deep-fry for 5 mins.

Chef's Tips

● to improve flavour, soak escalopes in a marinade of oil, lemon juice, and a crushed clove of garlic.
● a quick way to cook the meat is to cut the escalopes into thin strips. If you do this, serve with cooked sliced peppers and a little cream, to which some Worcester sauce has been added.

43

Roast Guinea Fowl

Ingredients

guinea fowl (2½lb / 1.25kg)
butter (2oz / 50g)
oil 2 Tbs
carrot 1 medium
onion 1 small

celery 2 sticks
bouquet garni 1
mace a pinch
salt and pepper to taste

Gravy:

bacon 1 rasher
giblets of guinea fowl

dry sherry (2fl oz / 50ml)
water (½pt / 300ml)

Preparation time 15 mins   **Cooking time** 40-45 mins
Portions 4   **Calories per portion** 394

Method

1 Wash and dry the bird, then season inside and out with salt, pepper, and mace. Smother the breast and legs with butter.
2 Peel the carrot and onion, and cut into small cubes. Dice celery. Heat some oil in a pan, and brown vegetables for 1-2 mins. Place vegetables in a casserole.
3 Preheat oven to 400°F / 200°C / Mark 6.

4 Dice bacon. Wash giblets, put them in a pan of cold water, and bring to boil. Rinse in cold water and drain. Add them to the vegetables with the bacon and the bouquet garni.

5 Place the guinea fowl in the casserole dish, cover with a lid, and roast for 20 mins. Remember to turn bird round so it cooks evenly. Remove lid after 20 mins in order to allow the bird to brown, add sherry, and cook a further 15 mins.

6 Remove bird, and leave to stand for 15 mins. Carve into portions. Pour contents of the casserole into a saucepan with water and boil for 15 mins. Strain the gravy and skim off fat; check seasoning.

7 Pour sauce into sauceboat, garnish the guinea fowl with some watercress, and serve with bread sauce and a green salad.

Variations

A Garnish the bird with button mushrooms and button onions, cooked separately for 8 mins.

B Joint the bird, and sauté pieces as you would chicken. Serve with game chips and salad.

C On removing from the oven, make a white sauce, and garnish with deseeded green grapes, which have been soaked for 5 mins in brandy.

Chef's Tips

● you can stuff the guinea fowl with sage and onion, or thyme, or apricots and then roast it.

● the gravy can be thickened by adding 1 or 2 teaspoons of cornflour, blended with ½ cup water, to the hot juices. Reboil for 4 mins until the gravy has a glossy appearance.

● the bird can be browned in a mixture of oil and butter in a fireproof casserole on top of the cooker. Turn it round until the surface is golden brown all over. The vegetables can then be browned in the same fat, the casserole covered with its lid, and the cooking process completed as described in the main recipe.

44

Chicken

With vegetables and a cream sauce, served with rice.

Ingredients

cooked chicken (1½lbs/720g)
white mushrooms (4oz/100g)
red peppers (4oz/100g)
onion chopped (1oz/25g)
oil 2 Tbs (1fl oz/25ml)
butter (1oz/25g)
sherry (2fl oz/50ml)
water (½pt/300ml)
chicken stock cube 1
double cream (2fl oz/50ml)
salt and **pepper** to taste
paprika a pinch
rice boiled or cooked as pilaff (10oz/275g)

Preparation time 10 mins   **Cooking time** 15 mins
Portions 4   **Calories per portion** 550

Method

1 Heat oil in a pan, and shallow-fry chopped onion, red
  pepper, cut into strips, and mushrooms, for 4 mins without
  browning.

2 Add the cooked chicken pieces, stir well, remove surplus fat, and pour in sherry, water, and stock cube. Boil for 10 mins.

3 Stir in cream, season to taste and boil for a further 4 mins.

4 Serve on a shallow dish with boiled rice or rice pilaff.

Variations

A Substitute strips of celery and white leeks for the peppers, and instead of sherry use white wine.

B Omit mushrooms and cream, increase the amount of red peppers and garlic but also add 2 Tbs tomato purée, and sprinkle with some chopped tarragon.

C Omit sherry and replace with pineapple juice, flavoured with chopped fresh ginger, garlic, and 1 Tbs soya sauce.

Chef's Tips

- basic ingredients can also be used for a pie filling or for vol-au-vents.
- try to use a good stock to make sauce. This gives more flavour.
- substitute turkey for chicken.

45

Chicken and Honey Chinese-Style

Fried chicken pieces, marinaded in spices, honey, and sherry.

Ingredients

chicken 1 roasting (3½lb/
    1¾kg)
salt 3 Tbs

mixed spice 1 tsp
black pepper ½ tsp

Stock:

water (3pts/1.8 litres)
soya sauce 1 cup (5fl oz/
    150ml)

ground ginger ½ Tbs
garlic 2 cloves, chopped
salt and pepper

Honey Marinade:

liquid honey 2 Tbs (1fl oz/
    25ml)
dry sherry 8 Tbs (4fl oz/
    100ml)

mixed spice 1 tsp
soya sauce 1 Tbs
oil 1 tsp
oil for deep frying

Preparation time 40 mins   Cooking time 10 mins
Marinading time 2 hours
Portions 4   Calories per portion 650

Method

1 Heat 3 Tbs salt, 1 tsp mixed spice, and ½ tsp black pepper in a pan for 2 mins to develop flavour. Remove and keep in a small container.
2 Prepare stock. Place water in a large pan, together with all the stock ingredients, and bring to the boil.
3 Cut chicken into 4 portions, and immerse in boiling stock for 2 mins. Remove stock from heat, with chicken, and allow to cool for 25 mins. Drain chicken.
4 Combine all marinade ingredients in a bowl. Place chicken pieces in a bowl and baste with marinade. Leaye for 2 hours, basting often.
5 Heat a cup of oil in a pan until smoking hot, and fry chicken pieces, 1 or 2 at a time, basting with fat. Cook for 5 mins. Drain well.
6 Serve with a garnish of boiled rice and raw fresh spring onions, together with the flavouring spices prepared in paragraph 1.

Variations

A Boil chicken pieces for 10 mins. Remove skin, cool, pass in beaten egg and breadcrumbs, and fry until golden brown.
B Rub the chicken with the same marinade, and roast for 35-40 mins at 350°F/180°C/Mark 4 until cooked. Cover with a lid for the first 30 mins to prevent the chicken browning too quickly.
C Use duck instead of chicken, but remember that the amount of meat on a duck is not as great as a chicken, so that you will require a bigger bird.

Chef's Tips

● if soya sauce is not available use Worcester sauce or 2 stock cubes crumbled in hot sherry, together with 1 additional Tbs of vinegar.
● the Chinese often colour their chicken red. If you wish to do the same add some cochineal standard red colour to the marinade.
● experiment with different spices — paprika, ground ginger, chilli powder, cinammon, cloves, nutmeg, garlic, ground thyme — until you hit on the flavour you like best.

46

Fried Chicken Maryland

Deep-fried chicken breasts with corn fritters.

Ingredients

chicken portions 4 breasts, with skin removed
egg 1 medium
breadcrumbs (3oz/75g)
flour 1 Tbs
salt and **pepper** to taste
oil for frying

Corn Fritters:

flour 1 cup (3½oz/90g)
egg 1 medium
milk ½ cup (4fl oz/100ml)
sweetcorn (4oz/100g)
baking powder 1 tsp

Garnish:

bananas 4
butter for frying

Preparation time 15 mins   **Cooking time** 8-10 mins
Portions 4   **Calories per portion** 675

Method

1 Beat an egg, and put it in a shallow bowl. Season the flour with salt and pepper, and roll chicken portions in it. Then roll them in beaten egg, and dip in breadcrumbs.
2 Heat oil to 375° F/190° C, and deep-fry chicken for about 8-10 mins. When cooked, drain and dry, and keep warm.
3 **Corn fritters:** mix the flour, salt, and baking powder; then beat egg, and add milk and a pinch of pepper. Add egg mixture to flour slowly, until you have a smooth batter. Dry the sweetcorn, and add to batter. Heat oil in a pan, and pour in 2-3 Tbs mixture at a time to make fritters. Cook until golden brown, then drain well.
4 Slice bananas lengthways, and fry gently for about 3 mins. Serve the chicken with corn fritters and bananas.

Variations

A Instead of frying in breadcrumbs, pass chicken pieces in batter.
B Add red and green peppers to the fritters.
C Cook breasts of chicken in a little oil, coat with chopped nuts, and serve with asparagus tips.

Chef's Tips

- use oil for cooking fritters; you get a much better result than butter or margarine.
- when making fritters, do not make the batter too thick.
- try and serve this dish as soon as it is cooked.
- chicken pieces can be shallow fried in a pan instead of deep fried. If you use this method, it is best to fry them for 4-5 mins only and then to bake them in the oven for 8 mins at 380° F/200° C/Mark 5. If kept in the frying pan, they can become too brown.

47

Boiled Chicken

Served with rice in a creamy sauce.

Ingredients

chicken 1 boiling fowl
  (4-5lbs/2-2½kg)
onions 2 small
cloves 4
celery 1 bunch (1lb/450g)

leeks 2
carrot 1 large
thyme a sprig
peppercorns 6

Thickening:

margarine (3oz/75g)
flour (3oz/75g)
finished stock (2pts/1¼litres)

single cream (¼pt/150ml)
lemon juice of half

Garnish:

onion 1 medium (2oz/50g)
butter (2oz/50g)
rice thick grain (8oz/225g)

chicken stock (1pt/600ml)
salt and pepper to taste
nutmeg grated, a pinch

Preparation time 15 mins   **Cooking time** 1½ hours
Portions 8   Calories per portion 635

Method

1 Place the bird in a large pot (8-pt/4-litre capacity) with

4pts/2litres of water. Bring to the boil, and remove scum as it rises, until the liquid is clear.

2 Prepare vegetables — stud onions with 2 cloves each, divide celery into four, cut carrot in half, clean leeks.

3 Add vegetables to chicken. Add herbs and peppercorns.

4 Simmer until bird is cooked. Remove any surplus fat floating on top. Lift the chicken out and cut into portions. Place in a shallow dish.

5 Prepare the rice during the last 30 mins of chicken cooking time. Heat a little butter in a pan, gently fry chopped onion for 4 mins, then stir in the rice for 1 min or so before adding chicken stock (1pt/600ml). Bring to the boil, cover with a lid, and simmer for 17 mins.

6 Prepare the sauce: heat margarine, and blend in flour. Cook for 2 mins without browning, and gradually add 2pts/1200ml stock to make a smooth sauce. Boil gently for 15-20 mins and then blend in cream. Season with salt and pepper, grated nutmeg, and the juice of half a lemon. Pour sauce over the chicken or serve separately.

7 Arrange carrot and celery as garnish round chicken and serve with the rice.

Variations

A Instead of celery and leeks use 6 small leeks to flavour the stock.

B Make a richer sauce by adding 2 egg yolks with cream, and add some grated lemon rind, as well as the juice of 2 lemons.

C Instead of rice use some pasta.

Chef's Tips

● surplus stock can be made up into soup, or used for other sauces.

● boil the chicken gently — this will help to tenderise the meat.

● any left-over chicken can be fried up the next day with rice to make a pilaff. Or dice any left-over meat, mix with sauce, and use as a filling for pies or a quiche.

48

Chicken and Apricot Curry

Ingredients

chicken 4 portions
oil 4 Tbs (2fl oz/50ml)
onion 1 large, sliced (4oz/100g)
garlic 2 cloves, crushed
tomato purée 1 Tbs
dessicated coconut 1 Tbs
water (¾pt/450ml)
apricots fresh or canned (8oz/225g)
cornflour 2 tsp to thicken sauce
water ½ cup to blend with cornflour
salt and **pepper** to taste
curry powder 3 tsp

Preparation time 15 mins   **Cooking time** 30 mins
Portions 4   **Calories per portion** 390

Method

1 Heat oil in a metal casserole and shallow-fry the chicken pieces until brown.
2 Add the onions and cook for 3 mins, then add garlic and curry powder. Turn over the chicken pieces, and, after 1

min, add the water and all other ingredients except apricots, cornflour, and ½ cup of water.

3 Simmer the chicken in the oven for 30-40 mins with a lid on.

4 Remove from heat, and thicken the sauce with cornflour and water mixed to a slurry. Boil for a further 4 mins.

5 Serve with a garnish of boiled rice — allow 2oz/50g per portion.

Variations

A Flavour the curry with 2oz/50g of hot mango chutney. Alternatively you can serve this cold at the table.

B Vary the fruit — use pineapple, apples, or peaches in the same quantity.

C You can hot up the sauce with the addition of ¼oz fresh chopped ginger and 1 chilli pepper.

Chef's Tips

- if using fresh apricots, remember to remove the stones.
- to add colour to rice, either add 2 tsp turmeric powder per 8oz/225g rice or a pinch of saffron.
- if you are short of time, cut up the chicken into smaller pieces — they will take less time to cook.
- remember that the flavour of the spices will be greatly enhanced if you stir-fry them with the chicken.

49

Chicken and Leek Pie

Layers of chicken and leek, covered with a puff pastry lid.

Ingredients

roasting chicken 1 medium (3¼lb/1.3kg)
onion 1 medium
carrot 1 medium
leeks 8 small (8oz/225g)
salt and **pepper** to taste
white wine (½pt/300ml)
puff pastry fresh or frozen (1lb/450g)
egg yolk 1
bouquet garni 1
thyme a pinch

Preparation time 20 mins   **Cooking time** 1 hour
Portions 6   **Calories per portion** 600

Method

1 Joint the chicken into 10 pieces, without the bones. Clean and wash the leeks. Slit the bottoms. Clean and slice carrot and onion.
2 Prepare a stock. Wash giblets and then scald them in boiling water. Drain, and place in a saucepan with 1pt/600ml

water. Add onion and carrot, bouquet garni, and thyme. Boil for 35 mins. Strain and then leave until cold.

3 Place the chicken pieces in a 3½-pt (2-litre) pie dish. Alternate with slices of leek. Season and then pour in the stock and white wine.

4 Roll out pastry to ⅛in/2mm thickness. Cover the chicken. Brush with egg yolk or beaten whole egg. Rest pie for 2 hours. Brush with beaten egg again, and bake in a moderate oven for 45 mins-1 hour at 375₉F/190°C/ Mark 5. After 30 mins cover pastry with foil to prevent burning.

5 Serve hot or cold.

Variations

A Use onions instead of leeks, and thicken stock with a little cornflour and double cream (4fl oz/100ml)

B To the basic recipe add strips of celery and shredded cabbage.

C Omit white wine, and replace it with a fruit juice of your choice.

Chef's Tips

● resting pastry for 2 hours before baking prevents it from shrinking. If you are short of time use short crust pastry instead — this does not need to rest.

● wine in this recipe can be replaced by water, but, if so, it is essential a good stock is used.

● if there is any pastry left over, use it to decorate the top of the pie.

● boiling fowl are tougher — but cheaper — so, if you use one, do cook it first in stock. Then skin and dice it and bake with the leeks as in the main recipe. The leeks need not be precooked as their flavour develops better during the baking process than if they are boiled.

50

Rabbit Casserole

Sautéed rabbit with mushrooms and herbs in white wine.

Ingredients

young rabbit 1 (3lbs/1½kg)
butter 2 Tbs (1fl oz/25ml)
oil 2 Tbs (1fl oz/25ml)
onion 1 medium, chopped
  (2oz/50g)
garlic 1 clove, crushed
tarragon 2 fresh sprigs or 1
  tsp dried

thyme a pinch
bay leaf 1
dry white wine (¼pt/150ml)
water (½pt/300ml)
white button mushrooms
  (4oz/100g)
parsley 1 Tbs
salt and **pepper** to taste

Thickening:

soft butter 1 Tbs
flour 1 Tbs

Preparation time 20 mins   **Cooking time** 1 hour
Portions 6   **Calories per portion** 335

Method

1 Cut rabbit into 10 pieces (each hind leg into 2 pieces, the
  saddle and neck into 4). Save the heart and liver.
2 Season the pieces and dust them with flour.

3 Heat oil and butter in a casserole dish, and brown the rabbit pieces evenly; add the chopped onion and garlic. Cook for 4 mins.
4 Stir in the wine, water, and bay leaf. Bring to the boil and gently simmer for 30 mins. Remove scum as it rises. Add thyme and tarragon, and cook for a further 25 mins on a low heat. Cover with a lid to prevent evaporation.
5 Clean mushrooms, and add to the casserole 10 mins before the end of the cooking time.
6 Remove all the meat and the mushrooms from casserole into another dish.
7 Cream the butter and flour to a paste, and dilute with liquid to make the sauce. Whisk gently and boil for 8 mins. Check seasoning.
8 Sauté liver and heart for 3 mins, and add to meat.
9 Strain sauce over rabbit pieces. Sprinkle with chopped parsley.
10 Serve with a garnish of new potatoes and carrots.

Variations

A Instead of wine you can also use cider or beer, or even apple juice.
B Add 2oz/50g of the following vegetables — carrot, celery, parsnips, turnips. Put these in at the same time as onion.
C For a richer flavour add 1 Tbs tomato purée and replace the mushrooms with baked beans — add them at the last minute. Also add diced bacon (2oz/50g).

Chef's Tips

● try and use fresh herbs, especially chives, marjoram and sage, whenever possible — they do have more flavour.
● if you want to prepare a hare casserole, the preparation is the same, but the hare should be marinaded for at least 3 hours in wine, water, and vinegar before cooking. The vinegar should constitute 10 per cent of the total liquid.

51

Kidneys Sauteed in Wine and Armagnac

Ingredients

calves' kidneys 4
water (8fl oz/225ml)
vinegar 2 Tbs (1fl oz/25ml)
flour 2 Tbs (1oz/25g)
salt and **pepper** to taste
butter (3oz/75g)
onion 1 small, chopped
armagnac (2½fl oz/70ml)
white wine (3fl oz/75ml)
dijon mustard 1 tsp
double cream 3 Tbs (2fl oz/50ml)
parsley 1 tsp chopped

Preparation time 40 mins   **Cooking time** 15 mins
Portions 4   **Calories per portion** 565

Method

1 Remove the skin and membrane from the kidneys. Cut out the fat. Slice the kidneys across thinly, and soak in the vinegar and water for 30 minutes.

2 Drain and dry the kidneys and pass in the flour, which has been seasoned with salt and pepper.

3 Heat the butter in a pan, and sauté the kidneys and onion for about 5 mins. Pour in the armagnac, and set it alight. Pour in the white wine to put out the flames.

4 Simmer for 5 mins, and then strain off the juice into a saucepan. Keep the kidneys warm in the oven.

5 Bring the juice to the boil, and stir in the cream. Boil for a couple of minutes.

6 Blend together the mustard and lemon juice, and mix with sauce after removing from heat. Check the seasoning, and add the kidneys. Heat gently without boiling.

7 Serve on croûtons of fried bread, and sprinkle with chopped parsley.

Variations

A Omit the armagnac, and use ordinary brandy, and add sliced white mushrooms to the mixture (4oz/100g).

B Add some chopped tomato pulp (4oz/100g). Use vermouth instead of white wine.

C Use sherry and brandy, instead of wine and armagnac. Also add 1 shredded red pepper.

Chef's Tips

● to get rid of the smell from kidneys, wash in cold water mixed with 10 per cent vinegar before cooking.

● ox kidneys are best used with beef for stewing, and lamb' kidneys are best for grilling.

● be careful not to boil sauce after adding kidneys. Reheating kidneys toughens them.

52

Kidneys Sauteed

With button onions and mushrooms.

Ingredients

sheep's kidneys 8 (1lb/450g)
oil 4 Tbs (2fl oz/50ml)
button onions (8oz/225g)
button mushrooms (8oz/225g)
flour 1 Tbs
tomato purée 1 Tbs
red wine (5fl oz/150ml)
stock cube ½
salt and **pepper** to taste
ground thyme and **mace** a pinch of each

Preparation time 15 mins   **Cooking time** 15 mins
Portions 4   **Calories per portion** 300

Method

1 Skin the kidneys, cut each into half and discard all fat and
   sinews. Wash mushrooms and leave whole; peel the onions.
2 Pass the kidneys in seasoned flour, and brown quickly
   for 5 mins in a pan with half the oil. Keep hot in a
   casserole dish.

3 In the same fat, brown onions and mushrooms, and, when cooked, transfer them to a separate pan. Cover with red wine, add herbs and spices and stock cube. Stir in tomato purée and boil for 8 mins.
4 Add kidneys to sauce; reheat and simmer gently. Strain the sauce, and thicken with 1 tsp cornflour blended with 3 Tbs water.
5 Serve the kidneys in the sauce, with rice pilaff, or boiled new potatoes.

Variations

A The sauce can also be made with beer or cider or with just water and a stock cube.
B Use kidneys as part of a mixed grill, with liver, bacon, chops, and sausages. Omit sauce or serve it separately.
C Serve kidneys with a garnish of scrambled egg. Omit the sauce.

Chef's Tips

● if you find the smell of kidneys offensive, soak them for 15 mins in water and 10 per cent vinegar.
● remember not to overcook kidneys. Like liver overcooking toughens them. When reheating kidneys in sauce do not allow the mixture to boil.

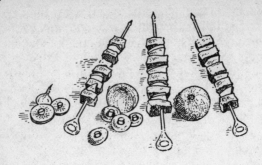

53

Marinaded Liver Kebabs

Liver pieces marinaded in yoghurt, threaded, with onion, on skewers, and grilled.

Ingredients

lamb's liver (2lbs/900g)
plain yoghurt (5fl oz/150ml)
salt and pepper to taste
flour (2oz/50g)
curry powder 1 tsp
oil 6 Tbs (3fl oz/90ml)
onions 2 large (8oz/225g)

Preparation time 45 mins   Cooking time 8 mins
Portions 8   Calories per portion 300

Method

1 Cut liver into ¾-in/2-cm cubes. Cut onions into four, and then separate quarters into layers.
2 Combine yoghurt with curry powder.
3 Marinade liver in yoghurt for 30 mins. Dry well. Pass in seasoned flour.
4 Dip liver pieces in oil, and impale on skewers. Alternate with onion pieces. Grill for 8 mins, basting with oil from time to time.
5 Serve with salad.

Variations

A The flavouring of the marinade can be changed. Try 1 cup of sherry with the juice of 1 lemon and 2 Tbs soya sauce. Also add 1 clove of crushed garlic and a pinch of ground ginger.

B A simpler flavouring would be to sprinkle Worcester sauce over the kebabs, and to alternate meat with mushrooms or bacon pieces.

C Use any other type of liver except ox liver.

D Wrap some chicken livers in slices of bacon; impale on skewers, and deep-fry for a few minutes.

E Pass liver in flour, dip in beaten egg and breadcrumbs, and then deep-fry until golden brown. Serve with salad.

Chef's Tips

- liver must not be underdone — but the longer it is cooked the tougher it gets.
- Sprinkle either coriander or caraway seeds over the meat before grilling.

54

Tripe and Onion

In a creamy white sauce.

Ingredients

tripe part reticulum or honeycomb (2lbs/950g)
water (1pt/600ml)
onion 2 large, sliced (8oz/225g)

Thickening:

margarine (1oz/25g)
flour (1oz/25g)
milk (½pt/300ml)
salt and **pepper** to taste
ground nutmeg a pinch

Preparation time 25 mins   **Cooking time** 2 hours
Portions 8   **Calories per portion** 350

Method

1 Wash well, and cut the tripe into 2-in/5-cm squares or
   into strips. Parboil in water for 15–20 mins and then
   refresh in cold water.
2 Drain, and place tripe in a saucepan with 1pt/600ml of
   water and the sliced onion. Bring to the boil, and stew gently
   for 1–1½ hours until tender.

3 Heat margarine and stir in the flour to make a roux. Gradually whisk in the cold milk, and then add ½pt/300ml of tripe stock to thin the sauce. Season.
4 Drain the tripe but save the stock in case you want to make the sauce thinner. Blend the white sauce to the tripe.
5 Serve with boiled new potatoes.

Variations

A Place the tripe in a shallow dish with layers of carrots and onions (½lb/225g each). Cover with dry cider. Add a bouquet garni, cover with a lid, and bake for 4 hours on a very low heat.
B Cut the tripe into thin shreds like noodles, and use white wine, instead of cider or milk. Add oregano, mint, and sage to flavour. Also put in some garlic and 2 Tbs tomato purée.
C When tripe is cooked in cider, it can then be minced, and used as a pâté or brawn. Add ½lb/225g diced beef to enrich the dish. Increase the cooking time by 1 hour.

Chef's Tips

● tripe — the cow's stomach — is very nourishing. It has a protein content of 18 per cent, and is very suitable for people who are ill.
● try blending with other stewing meats as an economy measure.

55

Stuffed Hearts

Lambs' hearts stuffed with sausage meat and herbs.

Ingredients

lambs' hearts 4 (8oz/225g each)

Stuffing

white breadcrumbs (3oz/75g)
sausage meat (3oz/75g)
egg 1 medium
onion 1 small
parsley, chopped 1 Tbs

dried sage and **thyme** a pinch of each
salt and **pepper** to taste
lemon juice and grated rind of 1

Sauce

oil (2fl oz/50ml)
onion 1 small (2oz/50g)
carrot 1 medium (2oz/50g)
stock cube 1

water (1pt/600ml)
celery 1 stick
tomato purée 1 Tbs

Thickening

cornflour 3 tsp
water ½ cup
salt and **pepper** to taste

Preparation time 20 mins   **Cooking time** 2 hours
Portions 8   **Calories per portion** 287

Method

1 Remove the tubes and excess fat, and enlarge the opening near the top for the stuffing.
2 Chop the onion, and blend all stuffing ingredients together. It should not be too crumbly.
3 Fill each heart to the brim with stuffing. Tie up the opening, and then season the outside.
4 Brown the hearts in a little fat, in an ovenproof casserole dish. When brown add a small onion — peeled and split in two — a split carrot, stick of celery, water, and a crumbled beef stock cube. Add 1pt/600ml of boiling water in which the tomato purée has been diluted. Cover with a lid and braise gently in the oven for 2 hours at 325° F/170° C/Mark 3.
5 When cooked, remove hearts, and place them in a clean shallow dish. Pour liquid and vegetables into a saucepan, and boil for 5 mins. Add cornflour and water to thicken and boil for 4 mins. Check seasoning.
6 Cut the hearts in halves and serve with a mixture of root vegetables or green cabbage, and sauté potatoes.

Variations

A Other animals' hearts can be prepared in the same way. Ox hearts are bigger, and take another 1 hour to cook.
B Use heart meat in stews. Cut heart in strips and use as an alternative to kidney in steak and kidney pies.

Chef's Tips

● If you serve hearts without stuffing them, the usual way to handle them after cooking is to carve them into thin slices like a joint of meat.
● half-cooked rice can be used instead of breadcrumbs in the stuffing.
● surplus stuffing can be used to stuff marrows, tomatoes, or peppers.

56

Potted Hams

Ingredients

cooked boiled ham half lean, half fat (1lb/450g)
dry white wine (½pt/300ml)
white vinegar (2fl oz/50ml)
garlic 1 clove, chopped
black pepper a good pinch
salt to taste
parsley chopped 2 Tbs
tarragon leaves 1 Tbs
honey 2 Tbs (1oz/25g)

Preparation time 15 mins   **Cooking time** 30 mins
Portions 6   **Calories per portion** 140

Method

1 Dice left-over ham. Discard rind, and place in a large pan with wine.
2 Bring to the boil, and simmer for 30–40 mins.
3 Add vinegar and honey and leave to cool.
4 When cold, mince, and blend in fresh herbs. Check seasoning.
5 Place mixture in an earthenware pot and refrigerate.
6 When cold, slice and serve with salads.

Variations

A Use left-over beef instead of ham — stewing beef is particularly suitable. Add 2oz/50g chopped onions and gherkins instead of herbs.

B Use left-over chicken and ham in equal quantities. Replace the wine with the same quantity of sherry or cider.

C Use prawns instead of meat. Reboil with white wine and vinegar. Dissolve 1oz/25g of aspic gelatine in hot liquid to set the mixture.

Chef's Tips

- make sure that there is an adequate amount of fat in the meat. It will not set as well otherwise.
- the meat will normally keep for about 1 week in the fridge.
- if you use fish or prawns, make sure you eat the potted mixture quickly.

57

Home-made Garlic Sausage Salami

Ingredients

raw lean minced pork (½lb/225g)
raw lean minced beef (½lb/225g)
left-over raw meat (½lb/225g)
raw pork or ham fat (½lb/225g)
onions chopped (½lb/225g)
black peppercorns 8
garlic 4 cloves, chopped
salt (1oz/25g)
paprika ½ tsp
mace a pinch
eggs 2
flour (2oz/50g)

Preparation time 20 mins + 12 hours in freezer
Cooking time 1½ hrs
Portions 8   **Calories per portion** 469

Method

1 Mince all the meat twice, together with onions, garlic, and fat.

2 Blend smoothly to a paste, adding eggs and flour, together with seasoning.

3 Roll the mixture into a sausage 2½–3in/6–7½cm thick. Wrap in greaseproof paper and freeze overnight.

4 Next day wrap the salami in muslin cloth. Tie with string and allow to thaw for 3–4 hours.

5 Boil or steam for 1 hour.

6 Cool, and, when cold, unwrap.

7 Serve cold, in slices, with salad.

Variations

A Use equal amounts of chicken and pork, and instead of peppercorns, add diced red peppers.

B Use duck meat, liver, and pork in equal amounts. Flavour with the grated rind of 1 orange and 1 lemon.

C For a special flavour, add to the basic mixture 2 Tbs fresh chopped chives and parsley.

Chef's Tips

● this dish is an ideal way of using up left-over meat.

● for correct seasoning you should add salt in the proportion of 2 per cent of the total weight of meat. For pepper you need 0.2 per cent of meat weight.

● to produce a pink salami add ½ tsp saltpetre to the salt used.

58

Chicken Brawn

With diced ham and gherkins.

Ingredients

chicken cooked, diced (1lb/450g)
pigs' or calves' trotters (feet) (1lb/450g)
celery 1 stick
carrot 1 large
onion 1 large
water (3pts/1800ml)
salt and pepper to taste
chicken stock cubes 2
gelatine (1oz/25g)
vinegar 2 Tbs

Garnish:

pickled gherkin (2oz/50g)
red pepper diced (2oz/50g)
loose sweet corn (4oz/100g)

Preparation time 20 mins   **Cooking time** 2½ hours
Portions 8   **Calories per portion** 140

Method

1 Place pigs' or calves' trotters in a large pan. Add water.
2 Bring to the boil, and remove scum as it rises to the surface.
3 Simmer for 1 hour, then add peeled onion, carrot, and celery, together with the vinegar. Boil for 1 more hour, then strain and discard vegetables.
4 Remove meat from trotters, and dice.
5 Place the chicken and trotter meat in a saucepan. Add 1½pts/900ml of the stock. Reboil for 30 mins.
6 Dissolve gelatine in the liquid, and add garnish ingredients.
7 Pour mixture into a deep earthenware oblong dish. Chill until mixture sets.
8 When firm, slice, and serve with salads.

Variations

A Substitute turkey or ham for chicken, and vary the garnish by using diced carrots and peas.
B Boil a pig's head. When tender, dice the meat including the tongue. Strain stock, and boil 3 pints/1800ml until it evaporates to 2 pints/1200ml. Blend dices meats. Season; add 2 Tbs vinegar, cool and pour into a mould. Keep in fridge intil set.
C Substitute diced boiled meat for chicken. Garnish with diced pickled cucumber or olives. Allow to set, and slice when firm.

Chef's Tips

● its important to remember to skim off the scum in the early stages of boiling the trotters. Not only will the end result taste better, but the jelly will be clear instead of cloudy.
● you can always add some port or sherry for extra flavour.

59

Chicken and Potato Mayonnaise

Ingredients

chicken cooked, diced (8oz/225g)
potato cooked, diced (8oz/225g)
anchovy fillets 1 tin (2oz/50g)
onion chopped (2oz/50g)
olives 8

Mayonnaise:

egg yolks 2
mustard 1 tsp
salad oil (¼pt/150ml)
hot wine vinegar 1 Tbs
salt and **pepper** to taste

Preparation time 20 mins   **Cooking time** 45 mins
Portions 6   **Calories per portion** 315

Method

1 Combine in a bowl the diced chicken and potato. Chill.

2 Prepare the mayonnaise: take a 2pt bowl and in it mix together egg yolks, mustard, and a pinch of salt. Start whisking the mixture and add oil a drop at a time to avoid curdling the sauce. When the mixture is thick, add the vinegar and a pinch of pepper.

3 Blend in the meat and potato mixture.

4 Place in a bowl, and decorate with thin strips of anchovy fillet and sliced olives.

5 Serve cold on a bed of lettuce leaves.

Variations

A Use ham and chicken in equal quantities, and replace potatoes with diced mixed vegetables.

B To mayonnaise add 2 Tbs tomato ketchup. Omit chicken, and replace with cooked prawns or boiled white fish.

C Add 2 Tbs apple purée to mayonnaise, and replace chicken with diced boiled beef and 2oz/50g diced pickled cucumber.

Chef's Tips

● this dish depends heavily on a good mayonnaise, and the key to that is the way in which the oil is added to the other ingredients. The oil must be poured in a drop at a time at first, otherwise you will not get an emulsion. Place your thumb over the top of the salad oil bottle to ensure that the oil does not surge into the egg yolks. The process of emulsification is helped if the oil is tepid.

● if the mayonnaise does curdle, add ½ cup of cream or white sauce. Whisk and make do with the plain salad cream dressing that will result.

60

Bacon and Onion Roly-Poly

Boiled bacon and onion rolled inside a suet crust.

Ingredients

bacon boiled (1lb/450g)
onions sliced (8oz/225g)
parsley chopped 1 Tbs
salt and **pepper** to taste
mustard powder 1 tsp

Suet Paste:

self-raising flour (8oz/225g)
shredded beef suet or **margarine** (4oz/100g)
water (2fl oz/50ml)
baking powder 1 level tsp
salt 1 good pinch

*4oz S.R. Flour
4oz fresh bread and
crumb
is better*

Preparation time 20 mins **Steaming time** 45–60 mins
Portions 6 **Calories per portion** 429

Method

1 First prepare pastry by sifting flour, salt, and baking powder. Rub in fat and add water to obtain a firm dough.
2 Roll to a rectangle 10ins x 6ins/25cm x 21cm and to a thickness of ¼in/6mm.
3 Place thin slices of the bacon over the pastry, and cover with chopped parsley and slices of onion.
4 Roll up and wrap in greased paper, and then in foil. Tie with string, and steam for 45–60 mins.
5 Serve hot with a parsley sauce.

Variations

A Alternatively the roll can be baked in the oven for 45mins at 400°F/200°C/Mark 6. If you do this, do not wrap the roll in a cloth or foil.
B Vary the meat — combine ham with chicken and also add a few raw sliced mushrooms.
C A more filling meat mixture can be produced by adding to the basic recipe 4oz/100g sausage meat blended with 1 raw egg.

Chef's Tips

● this dish is at its best when served with mushy peas and boiled green cabbage.
● the pastry will be lighter if you use tepid water when blending flour and fat to a dough.
● for a better flavour use butter instead of margarine.

61

Farmer's Flan

Ham and chicken in a pastry case.

Ingredients

ham (8oz/225g)
chicken (8oz/225g)
peas cooked (4oz/100g)
onion raw, chopped (2oz/50g)
egg 1 raw
salt and **pepper** to taste
short plain pastry (1lb/450g)
egg 1, for glazing

Preparation time 20 mins   **Cooking time** 35–40 mins
Portions 8   **Calories per portion** 440

Method

1 Dice cooked ham and chicken into ½-in/1-cm cubes. Combine with peas and raw onion, and blend in egg. Season.
2 Roll pastry to ¼-in/6mm thickness and line an 8-in/20-cm mould with half the pastry.
3 Fill mould with mixture.
4 Cover mixture with the rest of pastry. Trim and seal.
5 Brush with half the beaten egg.

6 Bake for 40 mins at 400°F/200°C/Mark 6.

7 Serve hot or cold.

Variations

A To basic mixture add 2 sliced hard boiled eggs, as well as a whole raw egg to bind ingredients together.

B Instead of ham and chicken, use left-over veal and pork in equal quantities, blended with sliced apples and a raw egg.

C Use left-over fish, e.g. cod, salmon, tuna; add a few sliced olives, bind with a raw egg, and flavour with dill.

Chef's Tips

- when you use left-over meat be careful to cook it thoroughly to destroy bacteria.
- the addition of a raw egg helps to bind the mixture, and improves the texture.

Appendix

General Hints on Wine-Making

These two wine recipes, which produce wine suitable for both drinking and cooking, will save you a lot of money if you use them. But wine-making does have its problems. Here are some of them, and, hopefully, some of the cures as well.

Pectin haze

Take a sample of the brew. Mix 1 part wine to 4 parts methylated spirits. Stand for 30 mins in a warm room. If pectin is present you will see it in the form of jelly-like clots and strings or use Pectolase (available from chemists).

Cure: Treat the wine with 15g of pectozyme per 5 litres, and leave in a warm room for 1 week.

Sterilization

The use of sulphate in the form of Campden tablets (metabisulphate) is essential in order to keep equipment sterile. One Campden tablet and a pinch of citric acid (or 2 tablets if citric acid is not used) dissolved in 1 pint/600ml of cold water destroys bacteria and fingi most effectively. Do *not* dissolve the tablets in hot water because the heat will cause the gas to be released too quickly, before it has time to sterilise the utensils.

Starch haze

This occurs with grain wines or beers. Add a drop of

iodine to a glass of the brew. If wine turns blue, there is
starch present. To clear, add 10g amylozyme per 150 litres
of brew or 1g per 15 litres.

Yeast hazes

These are removed by filtration.

Lactic acid bacteria haze

Symptom: Silky sheen when the jar is shaken.
Cure: 3 Campden tablets of metabisulphite per 5 litres.

A small colony of yeast sometimes revives and starts a
second fermentation.
Cure: 2 tablets of metabisulphate per 5 litres.

Filtration as a cure should be avoided as it spoils the
flavour.

If you follow the following guidelines your wine should be
perfect:
1 Keep the juice to be fermented at a regular temperature.
  Any fluctuation in temperature will affect the activity of
  the yeast.
2 Keep fermenting wine in a dark place. Ultra-violet light
  kills yeast.
3 Do not allow the temperature to fall below 66°F/19°C as
  fermentation will stop altogether.
4 Racking should not be done until after fermentation. To
  rack, syphon liquid from one jar to another, leaving
  behind deposit or 'lees'.
5 Fortification: This is the addition of alcohol to a
  finished wine to turn it into an aperitif. Fortification
  should be done before fining (see below).
6 Ageing: This is the rest period before bottling. The
  object is to eliminate undesirable smells and gases. Too
  much ageing in white wine tends to brown it. Ageing
  temperature should be between 50°F/10°C and 60°F/
  16°C. The normal ageing period is 6 months — 1 year.
7 Fining: If you only use grape juice, fining is not

necessary as the wine will clarify itself on resting. But with other juices it should be done either by filtration or with the use of a chemical agent such as Bentonite. After fining the wine should be undisturbed for 1 week.

8 Bottling: Do not bottle too soon. Only bottle when you are sure there is no more gas escaping from the brew.

Grape Red Wine

Ingredients

black grapes (5½lbs/2500g)
raisins (17oz/500g)
red grape concentrate (1lb/450g)
ammonium potassium 1 tsp
yeast culture (¼oz/8g)
water (6½pts/3 litres)
sugar (1lb/450g)

Preparation time 1 hour
First fermentation stage 10 days
Storing time 6 months prior to bottling
Calories per 4fl oz/100ml glass 125

Method

1 Remove stalks and then wash grapes in cold water. Drain, and squash with potato masher. Extract the juice, and collect the seeds and skin in a sterile bucket.

2 Boil water and scald raisins. Cool down to 80°F/27°C and add grape concentrate and juice. Dissolve sugar and add to bucket.

3 Add potassium. Cover bucket with a polythene cloth. Allow to ferment undisturbed at room temperature for 10 days. Strain into a clean gallon jar. Fit with air lock, and leave for a further 10 days until fermentation ceases.

4 Introduce a sterile glass tube into jar and siphon liquid into another jar. Leave behind deposit in bottom. This may have to be done twice until wine is clear.

5 Fit air lock with distilled water. Leave for another 20

138

weeks in the dark, or cover with a dark cloth.
6 Bottle and cork.

Chef's Tips

- leave the wine for at least 6 months before bottling. If bottled too soon, the corks may pop.
- if you want to increase alcohol content, take half the wine and place it in a plastic container with lid. Freeze until solid. The alcohol will separate and remain liquid. Collect and add to the wine. What is left behind can be used in a new batch.
- another method of increasing the alcohol content is to use 9oz/225g more sugar than prescribed in the list of ingredients.

Hock Wine

Ingredients

white grape concentrate (1lb/450g)
raisins (1lb/450g)
elderflowers (5oz/150g)
honey (1½lbs/720g)
ammonium potassium 2g
citric or tartaric acid (½oz/15g)
water (8½pts/5 litres)
Rudesheim yeast starter

Preparation time 1 hour
First fermentation stage 10 days
Storing time 3 months prior to bottling
Calories per 4fl oz/100ml glass 125

Method

1 Wash raisins, put them in a polythene bucket with a lid, and add 3½ litres of water at a temperature of 80°F/27°C.
2 Add grape concentrate and elderflowers.

3 Add acid and nutrient.
4 Check temperature and add yeast starter.
5 Leave at room temperature for 3-5 days.
6 Strain off the pulp and press slightly.
7 Dissolve honey with some liquid, and add to mixture.
8 Leave to ferment for 8 days at 70°F/20°C. Syphon juice to jar with airlock. Leave to ferment and rack.

Chef's Tips

● to turn this wine into a good aperitif, add a few drops of Angoustura bitters and place the dried skin of an orange in bottle. Leave for 2 weeks, and serve with ice cubes and mint leaves.

● try adding the syrup of canned fruit to finished wine.

● if you wish to try some of the wine before the recommended storing time has elapsed, rack some off into a screw-topped bottle and leave in the fridge for 24 hours before drinking or using it in cooking.

Index

Bold page numbers denote main recipes.